When Good Kids Make Bad Choices

ELYSE FITZPATRICK
JIM NEWHEISER
WITH DR. LAURA HENDRICKSON

HARVEST HOUSE PUBLISHERS

EUGENE, OREGON

Cover by Harvest House Publishers, Inc., Eugene, Oregon, Katie Brady, designer

This book contains the opinions and ideas of its authors, and is intended to provide helpful information on the subjects it discusses. The authors and publisher are not rendering personal medical, counseling, or pastoral services through this book. You should always consult with your personal physician, counselor, or pastor before making any decision about how to help a child with a specific problem. Medicines a child is already taking should *not* be stopped except under the supervision of a doctor.

WHEN GOOD KIDS MAKE BAD CHOICES
Copyright © 2005 by Elyse Fitzpatrick, Jim Newheiser, and Dr. Laura Hendrickson
Published by Harvest House Publishers
Eugene, Oregon 97402
www.harvesthousepublishers.com

Library of Congress Cataloging-in-Publication Data
Fitzpatrick, Elyse, 1950-
  When good kids make bad choices / Elyse Fitzpatrick and Jim Newheiser with Laura Hendrickson.
     p. cm.
Includes bibliographical references.
ISBN 0-7369-1564-8 (pbk.)
  1. Child rearing—Religious aspects—Christianity. 2. Parenting—Religious aspects—Christianity. 3. Choice (Psychology)—Religious aspects—Christianity. I. Newheiser, Jim. II. Hendrickson, Laura. III. Title.
BV4529.F56 2005
248.8'45—dc22   2004023925

Printed in the United States of America

05 06 07 08 09 10 11 12 13 / DP-KB / 10 9 8 7 6 5 4 3 2 1

To all our suffering brothers and sisters:
Your sovereign God is also a suffering God,
who knows the pain of losing a child
and who will walk with you through this heartache.
May His presence comfort and sustain you.

Acknowledgments

I would like to thank the parents who have shared their experiences with me in counseling and by filling out the survey. I admire the steadfastness of your faith, and your Christlike love for your kids. I would also like to thank my fellow elders and the members of Grace Bible Church for being so supportive of this project.

And, I would like to thank each of my sons for working hard that we might have a loving relationship. Most of all, I am grateful for my wife, Caroline, who has been a model of selfless love and unceasing prayer.

— Jim Newheiser

I am very grateful to George Scipione and Roger Wagner, my pastors and teachers, who taught me to think theologically about physical challenges. Physician-biblical counselor Michael Emlet's audiotape "My Body Made Me Do It?"—presented at the CCEF Living Faith 2002 conference—was foundational to my treatment of the body and the heart in Chapter 6. I also want to thank George Scipione, Jim Newheiser, and Steve Miller of Harvest House for special assistance in clarifying the message of chapters 6 and 7. Thanks also go to my best friend and colleague Eileen Scipione, who has always believed in me, to my faith family, who prayed faithfully for me, and to challenged counselees and friends too numerous to name who, along with their families, have taught me so much. I owe the greatest debt of gratitude to my dear husband Dan— thank you for all your love and support. And to my precious son, Eric— you are the reason for it all.

— Dr. Laura Hendrickson

I'd like to thank Jim Newheiser and Laura Hendrickson for undertaking this project and sharing their wisdom with me. Thanks, also, to George Scipione, the brains behind this project (at least for me!). Thanks also to my pastors (Mark Lauterbach and Craig Cabannis) and my home group at Grace Church (SGM), who prayed for me and excused me from my obligations so that I could work on this project. Thanks also to Steve Miller, my perpetual ally in the struggle to get biblical books into believers' hands. Thanks most of all to my family, Phil especially, who always understands and supports, and who will use this book with me as we counsel families together.

—Elyse Fitzpatrick

Contents

Our Dream Family

U ntil three years ago, our family was all my wife and I (Jim) had hoped it would be when we married in 1979. I would have been pleased to invite you into our home to meet our three children. We had much to be proud of. My wife had faithfully homeschooled our sons for 14 years. Our sons could have told you about their studies of the great books from a Christian perspective. You would have observed their willing participation in our family devotions. All of them were active in our church's youth group and in other profitable activities such as Christian worldview camps and summer missions trips.

I believed that every member of our lovely family was devoted to the church where I serve as pastor. I can fondly recall coming home after the evening service with my heart full of thanks to God and my family because we were of one heart serving Him together.

Two of our sons were National Merit Scholars with the ambition of using their gifts to serve the Lord. Our oldest son was attending a prestigious liberal arts college where he was involved in a sound church and an InterVarsity chapter. He had a good relationship with his pastor and the InterVarsity leader. And our second son was about to go off to a top-ranked engineering school.

If you had visited our happy home, you would have seen three young men who were polite, respectful, articulate, and helpful. We frequently practiced hospitality and you would have seen each member of our family participating in making you feel welcome. We were living the *godly Christian family* dream.

Our Dream Becomes a Nightmare

In light of all this, perhaps you can imagine our shock when our oldest son informed us that he no longer believed that Jesus Christ was the only way to God or that the Bible was authoritative. Although that phone conversation took place over three years ago, I still feel its aftereffects deeply. It was during this dark call that he told me he had left the solid evangelical church where we had settled him during his freshman year in college and joined a very liberal church which questioned or denied much of what he had learned. Furthermore, he told us that he had become involved in a serious romantic relationship with a Buddhist girl. For some time he had been hiding these changes from my wife and me, but then finally decided he needed to completely break away from us and live his life as he pleased.

The shock and heartbreak my wife and I experienced was unlike anything we had ever known before. Indeed, it seemed to me that up until that day, I could have taken all the tears that I had seen my sweet and cheerful wife shed over the past 25 years and put them in a thimble. Over the next several weeks, I would have needed buckets.

Especially hard was seeing these changes after we had worked so diligently to train our children up in "the discipline and instruction of the Lord" (Ephesians 6:4). My wife had devoted her entire adult life to training our children to serve God, homeschooling them so that our family would be the primary influence in their lives. Together we had prayed with them and for them, regularly leading them in our family devotions. We sought to prepare them for the intellectual challenges of college by sending them to Christian worldview camps and by teaching them to critique worldly ideology with a solidly God-centered philosophy. In addition, we also trained them in the biblical principles of sexual purity and courtship before marriage. But now our lives were consumed with trying to answer a question that haunted us: *How could this be happening?*

The Nightmare Intensifies

Our sorrow was further compounded when our youngest son, then 13, began to take the side of his older rebellious brother, buying into his argument that we were narrow and restrictive. He began to become alienated from us and our faith, and soon demanded that we stop homeschooling him so he could go to public school and be "normal."

My wife and I suffered through many sleepless nights, and when we finally were able to get some rest, we would wake up hoping that what we were experiencing had been merely a very bad nightmare.

Again, how could this be happening to us? Didn't Proverbs 22:6 say, "Train up a child in the way he should go; even when he is old he will not depart from it"? Hadn't we sought to give our children the best possible upbringing?

As we sought to examine ourselves, we wrestled in our own hearts with many doubts and fears. Our confusion was compounded as we listened to the opinions of well-meaning family members and friends. Some told us we had provoked our sons to rebellion by being too strict and demanding. Others said we had failed because we were too loose and allowed our oldest son to attend a non-Christian college. Some went so far as to suggest that our problem may have stemmed from exposing our children to various philosophies and worldviews in the homeschooling curriculum we had used.

We wondered if our sons' rebellion was our fault. *Did our kids turn away from our faith because we failed to live for the Lord as we should?* We would see other families with wonderful kids, those families that grace the covers of homeschooling magazines, and wonder, *What did they do right that we did wrong? Did we neglect our children? How could we have been so mistaken?* To further complicate our turmoil, we began to wonder if I was disqualified for pastoral ministry because our children did not embrace our faith (Titus 1:6).[1]

As we questioned whether Proverbs 22:6, the verse so many parents rely on, was a promise or a maxim, more questions surfaced. *Can we hope our rebellious children will eventually come back to the truth when they're older?* Many well-meaning friends told us they were "sure" our kids would come back around. Although we appreciated our friends' concern and desire to comfort us, we wondered whether there was any biblical basis for their certainty, or if their words of encouragement were just wishful thinking on their part.

A Nightmare Shared with Other Parents

All through the turmoil and rough times we have faced, we have been deeply blessed by the way the Bible speaks so openly about parents who suffered just like us. Think about it: the very first parents, Adam and Eve, had a wayward child, Cain, who turned not only from his family, but also rejected the counsel of the Lord Himself. The Bible is filled with the stories of good parents who had rebellious children, and also of negligent parents who had godly children. Within these stories we have received much comfort and answers to the questions that have plagued our souls.

In my ministry as a pastor and biblical counselor, I've also met other Christian parents with shattered dreams. I have met godly parents whose children had become involved in every form of worldliness, including drugs, alcohol, fornication, and even homosexuality. In fact, I've been amazed at how *many* Christian parents are hurting. So if you are in that same place, you are definitely not alone. In the pages of this book, we'll share what we and other Christian parents have grappled with and how it really is possible to have hope in the midst of great agony and despair.

My wife and I know what it's like to feel the censure of others who seem to be saying, "If you had just done things right like we are doing, you wouldn't be having these problems." I'll humbly admit that I was greatly convicted when I realized that at one time, I used to think such things in my heart—that is, *before* April 1, 2001. Instead of perhaps well-meaning but unhelpful criticism, you and I need the hope and encouragement which only God can supply, and this book will help you find it.

God Is Working All Things Together for Our Good

The psalmist said, "It was good for me that I was afflicted, that I might learn your statutes" (Psalm 119:71). *Good for me? Am I reading that right? How can that possibly be true when my child chooses to rebel and even turn his or her back on God?*

The Bible's perspective is certainly different than ours, isn't it? So, while my wife and I can't say that we have enjoyed the trials of the past few years, or that we would wish them on anyone else, we freely confess that we have seen the hand of God working in our lives. One blessing is that we have been humbled. Never again will we look at families whose kids rebel and think, *I wonder what they did wrong?* Instead, we have learned to show a more understanding compassion toward those who suffer all kinds of emotional hurts and betrayals. We believe God has blessed us with new sensitivity, insight, and empathy for others that we would have known nothing about if God had not allowed our dream to be shattered.

During this difficult season, my wife and I have also been blessed by the love and compassion of certain people whom God has placed in our lives. We have been amazed at how the people in our church and in the extended Christian community have been so kind and non-judgmental towards us. Countless brothers and sisters in Christ are praying for our kids. One couple even committed to regularly praying and fasting on behalf of our family. We now know the love and grace of the body of Christ as never before. We would never have experienced this were it not for our affliction.

In our suffering we've been blessed because we have learned to love others, especially our children, as God has loved us. This affliction has been good for us because it's causing us to learn more about the great self-sacrificing love of our Savior. We're learning to care about our kids even when we can't show them off to our Christian friends. We're making a genuine effort to understand them even when their beliefs are very different from ours, and to reach out to them even though they may not be seeking us. God is teaching us to be patient and kind even when we're provoked; and we're learning to communicate with people who speak what sometimes seems to us like a different language altogether. We've learned what it is to suffer and to feel as if the Evil One has beaten us to within an inch of our lives, but in every instance, we've learned of the Lord's power to sustain us.

We also believe that one of the greatest goods that can come from our affliction is the potential blessing this book might be to you. God, in His goodness, has already allowed our experiences to be a help to many others who are going through similar trials, and we trust that what we share in the pages ahead will sustain you and help you obtain the resources that God has provided for those who are enduring the troubles we've gone through. This is exactly what Paul referred to when he wrote 2 Corinthians 1:3-4: "Blessed be the God and Father of our Lord Jesus Christ, the Father of mercies and God of all comfort, who comforts us in all our affliction so that we will be able to comfort those who are in any affliction with the comfort with which we ourselves are comforted by God."

God's Word Has the Answers You Need

As my wife and I have wrestled through these issues, we have found hope, wisdom, and strength in the infallible and all-sufficient Scriptures. Joining us in our conversation with you is Elyse Fitzpatrick, a woman and friend who is also an author, biblical counselor, mother, and grandmother, and who knows the heartache of having a child turn from the truth. Dr. Laura Hendrickson, a former psychiatrist, has also joined us to share briefly about medical issues such as learning difficulties and prescription medications given to children. She will also share out of her own suffering as the mother of an autistic child.

As you can see, the counsel that you'll discover in this book isn't counsel that comes from writers whose families are perfect. *None of us is qualified to appear on the cover of a homeschooling magazine.* Although we've often wished we could turn the clock back to happier days, we've grown in our thankfulness to God for using our afflictions for His good purposes.

Not only is the counsel you receive in this book borne of our life experiences, but it is also firmly grounded in God's own advice for life, which is found in the Bible. Our desire is not to supply mere pious platitudes or impractical maxims, but counsel with substance and meaning that will answer questions like

- Why do our children turn out the way they do?

- What can we do to prevent our children from rebelling even more?

- What should we do when we sense that we are losing our kids?

- How can we communicate with a young adult who doesn't want to talk to us?

- Can anything be done with a young person who is completely out of control?

- What should we expect from children who have been diagnosed with learning disabilities or prescribed behavior-modifying medicines?

- How can we protect our marriage and our other children from the firestorm created by the rebellious child?

- How can we face the fear, shame, anger, guilt, and sorrow rebellious kids bring into our lives?

Let's Embrace a Different Dream

As we write this, we do so knowing that the stories of our families are not over yet. The Lord has done much to begin restoring our relationships with our kids. Channels of communication are opening up. And even though we're still in doubt as to their spiritual state, we're glad that there is a growing mutual love and respect. We are hopeful that God will yet bring back our children, but whatever realities we awaken to tomorrow, we are certain that the Lord will be our Help because He has promised to sustain us morning by morning.

So, we invite you to join us. If your dreams as a parent have become shattered, we want you to know that God's grace and mercy can reach into your life today, and that you can have hope for a better tomorrow—a tomorrow filled with comfort, peace, and hope because of God's great love and power.

PART ONE

Seeking
Comfort and Wisdom
As a Parent

1

Why Do Kids Turn Out the Way They Do?

Behold, children are a heritage from the LORD,
the fruit of the womb is a reward.
—PSALM 127:3

W hat was your heart's response when you read the verse above? Would you agree that children really are a gift from the Lord, a reward? Or to ask the question more pointedly, Would you say that *your* children are a gift or a reward from the Lord for you personally...or do you feel as if this is just a nice sentiment meant for someone else?

You might be thinking, *Yes, some of my kids are a gift, but not* that *child!* Or is your response a more emphatic, tear-drenched, "No!"? Maybe your sorrows have made you more cynical and you're beginning to wonder just what God means when He uses the words "gift" and "reward." Or perhaps you can remember a time when you did believe that your children were a gift, during those days when they were little and first smiled up at you with their sweet toothless grins. But now, darker images of angry, spiteful, and bitter words have obscured those beloved memories.

If you're nodding your head and thinking, *Yes, I'll admit it. I'm beginning to question God's promises and just what He's doing,* then let us encourage you: You're not alone. The writers of this book have each experienced the heartache you're living through—*you're not alone.* And even though the Bible tells us that children are a blessing, many other Christian parents are grieving over their kids today, just like you may be grieving over yours.

It just doesn't seem to make sense, does it? Children from "good homes" rebel against their upbringing. Teens raised in the church become involved with drugs, crime, sexual immorality, and gangs. Family relationships are in shambles as children tear apart the foundations their parents have lovingly sacrificed to build. Husbands and wives turn to each other and say, "I thought such things only happened to other people. This can't be happening to us! Where did we go wrong? What are we missing? Why is this happening?"

Our Shared Grief

Paul told the Corinthians that the temptations and trials they were experiencing were "common to man" (1 Corinthians 10:13):

> *No temptation has overtaken you that is not common to man.* God is faithful, and he will not let you be tempted beyond your ability, but with the temptation he will also provide the way of escape, that you may be able to endure it (emphasis added).

In part, what this verse means is that everyone faces deep heartache and sorrow at some time in their lives, and although others may not be suffering in the exact same way we are, we all share similar griefs and troubles. Yes, we all suffer temptations and trials. And many parents—even those mentioned in the Bible—

have experienced misery and sadness at the hands of their children, including the first parents, Adam and Eve.

The First Children

We're sure that Adam and Eve had high hopes for their two sons. They sought to raise their children to serve the Lord. While one son honored both God and his parents, the other was stubborn, self-willed, and hot-tempered. Ultimately this rebellious son murdered his younger brother and had to spend the rest of his life separated from his parents who loved him. Is it hard for you to imagine the anguish that Adam and Eve experienced? Probably not. The sad reality of life after Eden is that this story has been repeated in countless homes, including our own. Often, as in the first family, one child is obedient and godly, while another turns away from the faith and, by his actions, inflicts upon his parents shame, grief, and pain.

Many despairing mothers and fathers wonder why some children rebel as they do. Why is it that some families seem to have "perfect" kids, while others struggle? Does the answer lie solely in our way of parenting, or are there other factors at work?

Does Good Parenting Guarantee Good Kids?

There are some families who just exude sweetness and light, aren't there? These families walk into church with smiling faces, neatly dressed, and on time. The children are polite, respectful, and articulate with adults. Those of us who struggle with our children can be tempted to feel guilty, condemned, and incompetent in the presence of such success. When we see families like these, we wonder what they're doing right and we're doing wrong. We wonder what books they've read or what seminars they've attended. In fact, if you ask these parents the secret of their success, they'll usually tell you that if you would just follow the right formula (the one they follow), your kids would be just like theirs.

Are there "right" parenting formulas that guarantee you'll have godly children? For instance, some parents prefer a particular method of discipline. Others insist that a certain type of education is the key, while still others promote a particular curriculum that is *guaranteed* to instill godly character into children. These parents all believe that by carefully following a prescribed system, they will be assured of success. But are there really any failsafe methods of child-rearing? Does the Bible prescribe specific methods of parenting that promise success every time? The biblical answer to this question is *No, there are no foolproof methods of parenting.* That's because there are other factors at work in our children's lives, and because *none of us ever perfectly parents our children.*

Now, you may be wondering about certain Scripture passages that seem to say something different. We're aware of and we believe these passages too, many of them in Proverbs, so let's take a few moments now to consider them and the book of Proverbs in general.

Train Up a Child in the Way He Should Go

Proverbs 22:6 is a very familiar text, and probably one you've already thought of. It reads, "Train up a child in the way he should go; even when he is old he will not depart from it." This text does seem to prove the case of those who claim, "If you follow the right formula, you'll be a successful parent," doesn't it? It also seems to imply that those of us who have wayward children are solely to blame for their failure. Some people also take this verse to mean that even though our children might be straying right now, when they're older, they'll come back to God. But wayward children don't always come back—Cain didn't, did he? What, then, does this proverb mean? How should we understand it?

In order to understand the meaning of Proverbs 22:6, we need to grasp the nature of the proverbs overall. The book of Proverbs is not a collection of promises that will be fulfilled as long as the condition for the promise is met. Instead, the proverbs are *maxims* that wisely describe, in a general sense, the way that God has made the world to operate. For example, Proverbs 10:4 states, "A slack hand causes poverty, but the hand of the diligent makes rich." While it is true that those who are lazy generally come to poverty, we also see sluggards who win the lottery or inherit vast wealth. On the other hand, there are hardworking rice farmers in India who struggle to feed their families and would never even dream of having enough money to own a car. These exceptions do not invalidate the truth of this proverb; the maxim that hard work is profitable and laziness brings economic hardship is still wise and true and, *generally speaking,* proves applicable in most *but not all* cases.

In the same way, Proverbs 22:6 is a wise maxim. It is true that God often blesses godly parenting. Generally speaking, children from Christian families that honor the Scriptures usually turn out much better than children raised in unbelieving homes that reject His Word. There are, however, exceptions. Just as it's possible for a hardworking man to remain poor, it's also possible for kids who've had faithful parents to turn from the truth.

What we need to realize is that there are no promises that God will always and in every case save our children, no matter how diligent we are in directing them to the Lord we love. Take a moment now to breathe in the freedom and peace this truth brings you. Perhaps you have trained up your children in the way that they should go, and yet they're departing from it. Don't automatically assume that their rebellion is your fault. Consider instead the fact that the Bible teaches there are *three* factors, not just one, that determine how a child turns out:

- *Parents* are responsible to humbly honor the Lord and faithfully obey His Word in training their children.

- *Children* are responsible to humbly honor their parents and the Lord by responding in faithful obedience.

- *The Lord* is ruling sovereignly over the lives of both parents and children, directing them according to His good purposes.

Parents Are Responsible to Humbly Honor and Obey

Although it is true that God doesn't absolutely guarantee success in response to our faithful parenting, the Bible does make it very clear that *parents are responsible to train their children according to God's principles.* We are to diligently discipline our kids in the hope that God will work through our discipline and nurture to draw our children to Himself, as these Proverbs teach:

> Discipline your son, and he will give you rest; he will give delight to your heart (Proverbs 29:17).

> Do not withhold discipline from a child; if you strike him with a rod, he will not die. If you strike him with the rod, you will save his soul from Sheol (Proverbs 23:13-14).

We parents have an awesome responsibility, don't we? In fact, these verses make it clear that our parenting is so important it's a matter of life and death. The Lord encourages us to train our children because we might be the very means He will use to rescue our children from destruction and protect them from the foolishness that resides in their hearts.

How important is this responsibility? One example of a father's failure to lovingly discipline his children is given to us in the Old Testament. This father not only lost his ministry because of his neglect, but also his life.

Although Eli was blessed by God to be a priest and to offer sacrifices and prayers to Him, he's the classic biblical example of parental failure. He was overly permissive with his wicked sons, who were abusing their priestly prerogatives by eating forbidden portions of the temple sacrifices and committing acts of immorality with women who came to the temple to worship (1 Samuel 2:12-17). Although Eli asked his sons to change, he failed to take firm action to stop them. Instead of acting decisively, he just pleaded with and begged them to change. Because of his failure to restrain his children, God pronounced a serious judgment against his whole family: "I declare to him that I am about to punish his house forever, for the iniquity that he knew, because his sons were blaspheming God, and *he did not restrain them*" (1 Samuel 3:13, emphasis added).

It's easy to see why Eli responded as he did, isn't it? As parents, we often find it difficult to be as strong as we should be. Instead, we nag and hope that our son will eventually change or we leave our daughter alone and dream that she'll return to being the sweet girl she once was. Have you been guilty of failing to train your children as you should? Later in this book, we'll look at specific steps for you to take to re-institute godly parenting practices. But in the meantime, why not pause to speak with the Lord about your concerns and your willingness to recommit yourself to honoring Him, no matter what the cost?

Children Are Responsible for Their Decisions

Although parents are accountable to honor the Lord by faithfully training their children, *children are also responsible for their own decisions.* Godly parenting does not guarantee great kids because children make choices that are outside of our ability to control. Children are not merely robots or computers, but are human beings, created in the image of God with a heart and a soul. They can choose to follow or reject our ways because God created them with the ability to do so.

When our children were very young, we might have enjoyed the illusion of control. We were so much bigger, stronger, and smarter than they were that perhaps we foolishly thought that we could, with enough effort, compel them to follow our ways. But as they got older, they began to think for themselves and question whether or not they would embrace our choices. Then they gained more freedom and their sphere of relationships grew while our influence over them diminished. Although we were able to exercise some authority over their behavior when they were young, the truth is that their hearts have always been outside of our control.

The Child's Choice in Proverbs

The entire book of Proverbs is an appeal to a child to choose wisdom over folly. Even though the parent is telling him exactly what he needs to know (and doing so perfectly!), the child still must choose to respond in humble obedience. Having a wise father does not guarantee a wise son or daughter because a child can choose to reject the ways of wisdom and live foolishly. In Proverbs, wisdom and folly are portrayed as women who are trying to entice a young man to eat at their respective banquets (see Proverbs 9). The young person must choose where he will dine. His parent *can* counsel him but *can't* force him to dine at Wisdom's Table. And although he is young, his choices are very important. In fact, his reputation is based on his decisions, as Proverbs 20:11 teaches: "Even a child makes himself known by his acts, by whether his conduct is pure and upright."[1]

At whose table do your children usually dine? If you've been faithful to tell them about the delight of feasting with Wisdom, then their choice to eat the harmful fast food Folly offers is just that—*their choice.* Where they choose to dine has more to do with what they are hungry for than with how you've described what's on the menu. It's all about their choice.

Cain's Sad Choice

Have you ever wondered about the difference between Cain and Abel? They both had the same parents and the same upbringing. Cain's parents didn't have to contend with worldly influences, but he still rebelled, even though God Himself had graciously warned him to turn from his sin and choose the right way. Cain alone was responsible for his choice to reject God's counsel and kill his brother, and Cain bore the consequences of his sin (Genesis 4:11-12).

Israel's Rebellious Choice

Even the Lord Himself knows what it is like to be rejected by His children. Throughout the Old Testament, Israel is portrayed as God's son (Exodus 4:22; Jeremiah 31:9). The Lord was a perfect Father to His people. He delivered them from their enemies, planted them in a land flowing with milk and honey, and richly blessed them with His law so that they might prosper and enjoy His fellowship. But in spite of all this, Israel, God's son, rebelled and turned to other gods. When He lovingly disciplined them they didn't respond, but instead, hardened their hearts. Although no parents are as good and loving as our heavenly Father, we can probably relate to these heartbreaking words from the prophets:

> Children have I reared and brought up, but they have rebelled against me (Isaiah 1:2).

You have struck them down, but they felt no anguish. You have consumed them, but they refused to take correction. They have made their faces harder than rock; they have refused to repent (Jeremiah 5:3b-4).

Israel's rebellion was not caused by God's failure as a Father. It resulted from their wicked and foolish choices—and unhappily, they suffered the consequences of God's righteous judgment. Ponder now the truth that the Lord Himself understands the sorrow of having a rebellious son and remember...*you're not alone.*

Righteous Fathers and Wicked Children

In the book of Ezekiel, God makes it clear that children are responsible for their own choices. In a passage about righteous fathers who have wicked sons, God speaks of personal responsibility and accountability:

"If a man is righteous and does what is just and right— if he...walks in my statutes, and keeps my rules by acting faithfully—he is righteous; he shall surely live," declares the Lord GOD. "If he fathers a son who is violent, a shedder of blood, who does any of these things (though he himself did none of these things)....he [the son] shall not live....his blood shall be upon himself" (Ezekiel 18:5-6,9-11,13).

So, living as a godly parent does not ensure that your children will be godly. Children may, and sometimes do, choose to reject their parents' holy ways. And this passage clearly states that the Lord doesn't blame godly parents for the choices of their children, but rather, holds the children accountable.

The Spiritual Warfare in Our Homes

The battle for our families is actually spiritual in nature (Ephesians 6:12). The fundamental discord in our children's rebellion is not between them and us, but between our children and the Lord. When a child decides that he loves the world, he isn't just rejecting us; he's rejecting the things of God (1 John 2:15-17; James 4:4). As parents, we shouldn't be shocked (though we frequently are) that a child who loves the world may exhibit hatred toward us. Yet the Bible teaches, "Do not be surprised, brothers, that the world hates you" (1 John 3:13). And in Luke 12:51-53, Jesus said, "Do you think that I have come to give peace on earth? No, I tell you, but rather division. For from now on in one house there will be five divided, three against two and two against three. They will be divided, Father against son and son against Father, mother against daughter and daughter against mother...." Although a child's hatred is very painful, we are helped by remembering that this same hatred was experienced by our own dear Savior.

Rather than expecting that all children of all Christians will be saved, we should anticipate continued spiritual warfare and division until Christ returns, as John MacArthur writes:

> ...equipping a child with spiritual truth is no guarantee he or she will follow Christ. I know many diligent parents and grandparents whose hearts have been broken by a family member's rejection of Christ. We can only plant the seeds by teaching and living out the truth. How they respond is out of our hands.[2]

As you've read this chapter on children and their choices, we trust that your heart has been enlightened and your burden has been eased. Much of the sorrow we experience as parents of wayward children comes from the self-doubt and guilt we are prone to feel over our failures. *What did we do wrong? Did I love her too much or not enough? What did we say or fail to say that would have turned her heart?* We know all these questions because we've asked them ourselves. While we don't want to blithely excuse any possible failure on our part, we do want to help you recognize the difference between your responsibility and your children's.

The Lord Is Ruling Sovereignly

So far, we've looked at two of the three factors related to how our children turn out. Now it's time to look at the third: *The Lord is ruling sovereignly over the lives of both parents and children, directing them according to His purposes.*

From the standpoint of human responsibility, both parents and children make choices for which we are held accountable. Ultimately, however, we must rely on God to do, in our lives and in the lives of our children, what we are unable to do for ourselves. Psalm 127:1 says, "Unless the Lord builds the house, those who build it labor in vain." You know, the Lord has to pour out just as much grace to save a child from a believing family as He does to save one from a more worldly environment! We parents need to embrace this humbling (yet liberating) truth: *We are not in control of our children's destiny.* We are powerless to create faith in our children's hearts. While we can encourage our children to hunger for Wisdom's Feast, we cannot make that choice for them. Only the sovereign Lord can change our children's hearts, and that's because, as dear as they are to us, our children are sinners by nature.

Biblically Speaking, There Are No "Good" Kids

When you picked up this book and read the title, perhaps you did so because your heart resonated with the thought—*That's me!*

I've got a good kid (or at least she was raised to be a good kid!) who recently has made some pretty bad choices.

We may assume that our children are good because they aren't in serious trouble and they are reasonably compliant, but such an assessment is based on outward behavior and not the inner heart. We have to be very careful about saying, "My child may have made mistakes, but he really is a good boy." As much as we might want to believe that, we need to realize that ultimately, the question of "goodness" doesn't have to do with what we perceive or think, but whether our child truly has received Christ as his Savior. The Bible teaches that children are not good by nature; they are not a "blank slate" upon which we can write our values; they are not inherently innocent, nor are they genetically predisposed to be good. In fact, the Bible teaches that they are genetically predisposed to be bad because every child is born with original sin and a rebellious nature. This is the picture the Bible paints of our kids (and of us!):

> ...the intention of a man's heart is evil from his youth (Genesis 8:21).

> Behold, I was brought forth in iniquity, and in sin did my mother conceive me (Psalm 51:5).

> ...as it is written: None is righteous, no not one; no one understands; no one seeks for God. All have turned aside; together they have become worthless; no one does good, not even one (Romans 3:10-12).

These verses might seem hard for us to reconcile with our experience when we gaze upon our little darlings and see their halting attempts to obey us. Unbelieving children may be sweet and compliant on the surface because they've learned that compliance is in their best interest and they don't want to face the consequences of disobedience. This outward self-righteousness falls far short of true heart goodness (or righteousness) as defined in Scripture. True goodness is rooted in love for God and is motivated by a faithful desire to please and glorify Him (Colossians 3:17 and 1 Corinthians 10:31). Fear of consequences will not keep children from making sinful choices when they think that the consequences can be avoided, and as they grow older, their true nature will come out. Until God renews the heart, every child is dead in sin and unable to please Him.

> ...and you were dead in...trespasses and sins...(Ephesians 2:1).

> The mind that is set on the flesh is hostile to God, for it does not submit to God's law; indeed it cannot. Those who are in the flesh cannot please God (Romans 8:7-8).

You know, even if our children had perfect parents, the natural bent of their nature is to rebel. Remember the rebellion of Cain, the nation of Israel, and the prodigal son? Our children need God's sovereign grace for their nature to be changed. They'll never become "good" unless He changes them and then, of course, their goodness is not innate but rather imputed, because they've received the perfect righteousness of Jesus Christ and are being transformed by the Holy Spirit.

There Is Only One Perfect Parent

Often, when our kids rebel, we're tempted to become angry with God. We are tempted to seek to remind Him of our efforts, our sacrifices, our godly focus. We don't think that it's fair that our children are turning away from the Lord, especially when we compare our efforts to those of others who don't seem to be having any problems and who never really stood for the Lord the way we did. We think we deserve better. The fact is, however, that none of us "deserve" godly kids, because none of us have the power to change their hearts. None of us have been perfectly consistent in loving and disciplining them. And, like us, they are *saved by God's grace alone.* Only God can change your children, for salvation—and the transformation that results—is of the Lord.

Our Dysfunctional Homes

No one's home is what it should be because no one's home is free from sin. All of our homes are "dysfunctional" to a certain extent, because all of us fail to function in the ways that God has commanded, including our children. The good news is that God can overcome each of these problems through His Son. *God's sovereignty is our only source of hope—not our children, our parenting skills, our spouse, or even this book.*

The writers of this book are so thankful that we all serve a God who is able to turn the heart of a rebel back to Himself. He is able to forgive us for our failures as parents and to show mercy to our children. He is able to overcome our past transgressions and present difficulties. As you continue to study through this book, we trust that you'll gain hope and encouragement from His Word. And remember, you're not alone. He understands your heartbreak, and He'll help you every step of the way.

At the conclusion of every chapter, we're going to include some questions that you can use for personal study and practical application. If you choose to go through this book with a group, these questions will help spur you on to meaningful thought and further discussion. Please take time to complete them, and we trust that the Lord will use them to encourage and strengthen you.

Growing in Hope, Discovering His Help

1. Read 1 Corinthians 10:13. What are the promises found in this passage?

2. Before you read this chapter, what was your understanding of Proverbs 22:6? What is your understanding now?

3. What three factors influence a child's life-choices? Have you ever thought about them in this way before? Which one(s) are most meaningful to you?

4. Read Proverbs 9. How do wisdom and folly describe what they have to offer? In your own words, describe the difference and ask the Lord to give you an opportunity to share this truth with your children.

5. Have you thought that your kids were "good"? What does the Bible say about our true nature before salvation? What does the story of the prodigal son (Luke 15:11-32) teach you about parents and children?

6. So that you can more easily remember what you've learned, summarize it here in three or four sentences while it's fresh in your mind.

2

Their Choices, Our Tears

My God, I cry by day, but you do not answer,
and by night, but I find no rest. Yet you are holy,
enthroned on the praises of Israel.
—PSALM 22:2-3

I n the 1993 film *Shadowlands*, a student of C. S. Lewis told him, "We read so that we know we aren't alone"—a thought that Lewis echoes back with new understanding after the early death of his beloved wife, Joy. As you traverse through this book, we know you're with us for the same reason: *You want to know that you're not alone.*

And yet, in many ways, even as you see your struggles spelled out on these pages, you may still feel alone, isolated, and somehow different. For example, when you walk into church—a place that used to be an oasis filled with sparkling water and lavish fare—all you can see are the smiling faces of happy families with obedient children who unknowingly mock all your endeavors, all the love you poured out on your children. You may feel like you're dry and starving while everyone around you has rivers to splash in and food to the full. You may have friends who, like Job's comforters, are trying to help but only succeed in making you feel worse. "Just hang in there," they say. "God will help you." Or, perhaps their counsel to you is even more painful: "If you would just be more consistent (or loving, or disciplined, or God-centered, or faithful), your child would be like mine." These words and others like them can be like daggers that cut us to the heart and make us wonder if this dark night will ever end. *How can I hope? When will the dawn finally come?*

Shamed and perhaps embittered, you leave their company and drag yourself back home, to a place that once offered comfort and refuge for you and your family—only to be stricken again with the feelings of isolation and hopelessness. Everywhere you look you see the reminders of your heartbreak. Perhaps you still endure incessant quarreling and the relentless tears that have come to stay as an uninvited yet permanent boarder. Doubts about the veracity of your faith threaten to drown out the truths that once filled your soul with direction and hope. *When I call to God, does He hear me? Does He care how I'm suffering? Is He strong enough to help me? And if He is, why doesn't He? Does He really love me, or have I been fooled by my own desires to believe that there is Someone out there who cares for me?* And as you ask these questions, the enemy continues to attack you, bring up your failures, and show you others' successes. He deceitfully whispers in your ear, *You're alone. No one cares. God isn't real and if He is, He won't help you. Just give up…just give up…just give up.*

Our hope is that as you keep reading, you'll know you're not alone, because each of the authors of this book have first-hand knowledge of the pain you're experiencing, and we've also counseled many parents just like you. And yet while we want that truth to comfort you, we also recognize that it's not enough for you to know that we've experienced what you're going through. We realize we don't have the power to change your circumstances.

As the old saying goes, "Misery loves company," and that's true, but we don't want you to be just another miserable parent surrounded by other miserable parents. We know you need something more. You need Someone stronger who will lift you out of the muddy cisterns of sorrow and place your feet again on dry, solid ground. And that Someone is the Lord.

The verse that opens this chapter says, "My God, I cry by day, but you do not answer, and by night, but I find no rest. Yet you are holy, enthroned on the praises of Israel." Can you see how the author of this psalm encouraged himself? Like you, he was in great agony, but he comforted himself with truth about God's character: God is holy. In essence, we could paraphrase him as saying,

> My God, it seems to me that You aren't holding up Your part of the bargain. I'm crying to You, but You aren't answering me. Even though it seems like You're failing to be faithful, I'll remember this about You: You are holy—You don't sin, You don't mock my suffering. Instead of thinking low thoughts about You, I'll praise You for Your character.

Can you see what David was doing? He was choosing to look at his experiences through the lens of truth. Yes, your experience is hard. And yes, you may feel like you're alone in this. But the real truth is that God is holy and faithful, and He won't ever leave you or put you into a trial that is more than you can bear. Won't you take a moment right now to talk with the Lord about His faithfulness and holiness? Then ask Him for the grace to fill your heart with a song of love for Him. You can rejoin us when you're done.

Keeping Your Focus on God

As you traverse this rocky path, one of the most difficult lessons to learn is to keep your focus on God—especially since it's in times like this that the world will tell you to focus on yourself and your needs. Did shifting your focus from your unanswered prayers to God's good nature help you just now to regain hope? That's what this chapter is about: *keeping your heart and mind filled with truth about God*. So, as we share with you about overcoming despair, worry, fear, and anger, we're also going to continually direct you back to your only source of hope: God alone.

Have you ever noticed how your attention can be captured by a small but terrible pain? Even though your little toe isn't a major part of your body, when you ram it into the corner of the couch, your whole body is affected! For awhile, you aren't able to do or think about anything else as you hop up and down in pain.

That's how emotional pain is, too. It tends to overshadow any other thought as it demands your attention. Because what you're experiencing is so painful, you may be tempted to focus on your feelings, and yet those feelings themselves will obscure the very remedy that will ease your pain. Your pain may tell you to focus inward, and that's what you don't want to do. Instead of hopping up and down in great agony of soul, you want to focus on loving God and others. That may seem a puzzling answer to your heartbreak, but let's see why this really does work.

A Sorrow that Never Ceases

It's not uncommon for us parents to be filled with despair when our kids rebel. We feel devastated that our children are rejecting us and our values. Grief over a child who is lost to us is similar to the grief we would feel if a child had actually died. But grief from a rebellious child goes on and on and never seems to find a place of closure. It's not like we can go visit a grave and put flowers on it. Instead, this feels like an ongoing "death" and our grieving won't go away until our child has a change of heart. Because our hearts are filled with such woe, we can be tempted to crawl into a protective coffin of our own and withdraw from friends, other family members, and even God, pulling the heavy lid firmly down over us.

Our grief doesn't remain static, either. No, it grows. It grows because we water it with our tears, especially our tears of false hope. Each time we do something kind for our child, we think, *Surely now he will see how much I love him, and will love me in return.* When we pour out our hurt feelings to our daughter we imagine, *When she understands how she is breaking my heart, she'll come back.* When our son faces trouble we hope, *Surely this crisis will turn him around.* But as time goes by and the hoped-for change doesn't occur, we lose hope—again. On and on our despair grows, and like Job, we feel as if God Himself has turned against us. *Are You good? Do You love me, Lord?* Job's despair sounded just like this: "I cry to you for help and you do not answer me; I stand and you only look at me. You have turned cruel to me; with the might of your hand you persecute me" (Job 30:20-21).

A Shrub in the Desert

The prophet Jeremiah talked about feeling weak, dry, and barren in words that may seem familiar to you: "He is like a shrub in the desert, and shall not see any good come. He shall dwell in the parched places of the wilderness in an uninhabited salt land" (Jeremiah 17:6). Would you say that summarizes your experience? Desert, parched places, wilderness, uninhabited salt land—those are pretty dreary portrayals, aren't they? In this same passage, Jeremiah writes that the reason we feel this way is because we've turned away from the Lord and put our trust in man: "Thus says the LORD: Cursed is the man who trusts in man and makes flesh his strength, whose heart turns away from the LORD" (Jeremiah 17:5).

Hold on a minute! you might be thinking. *I'm not the one who turned away from the Lord—my child has done that!* We're not saying that you don't love the Lord or want to serve Him. What we do mean—and what the Bible tells us—is that despair and depression will result when your happiness is dependent on someone other than the Lord. Is your happiness dependent on your child? Are you trusting in him to bring you joy and peace? That's why he has so much power to shatter your heart. It's easy for him to dash your hopes and send you into a downward spiral of doubt and tears, isn't it?

On the other hand, if it seems to you that she's doing better, then life may seem lovely again and you may feel more like a well-watered garden. The built-in problem with putting our trust in people, and especially in our children, is that they'll let us down. People were never meant to be our primary source of joy. They are *a* source of happiness to be sure, but they aren't to be *the* mediators of our gladness. Jesus Christ is to be our source—not our spouse or our children or anyone else. It's Christ's peace and joy that we need.

What is the answer, then, to our despair, sorrow, and grief? Jeremiah tells us, "Blessed is the man who trusts in the LORD, whose trust is the LORD. He is like a tree planted by water, that sends out its roots by the stream, and does not fear when heat comes, for its leaves remain green, and is not anxious in the year of drought, for it does not cease to bear fruit" (Jeremiah 17:7-8). Look again at how this person's life is portrayed: gurgling brooks, calm assurance, flourishing growth in difficulty, and rewarding productivity. Wow! That's quite a different picture, isn't it? What is the difference? Is this person's life well-watered and delightful because he doesn't face any difficulty? No, that's not what the verse tells us. In fact, this person is facing heat and drought—biblical language for life's difficulties. But his response to difficulty is positive. Why? Because of where he has put his trust: *in the Lord.* The one who trusts God and bases his happiness upon his relationship with the Lord will flourish, even when others, including his children, fail him.

> Looking back upon my life, I realize that until April 2001, I was living in a rain forest. My wife and sons were a continual blessing and encouragement to me. When my time of drought came, my trust in God was tested, and initially I wilted into depression. I had to learn how to have joy in the Lord, even when what was most important in this life was falling apart all around me. During this time, I've discovered that a drought can be a good thing. It forces a healthy tree to send its roots deeper. I learned that when my children weren't giving me the watering I desired, I had to turn to God and trust Him more deeply than I ever had in my life.
>
> —Jim

In the midst of our trouble, we need to send our roots deeper into God by drawing closer to Him through His Word and prayer. The Psalms are a great encouragement for us when we're in trouble, because while they express the full range of our emotions, they always turn us back to the Lord our Helper. For example...

God is our refuge and strength, a very present help in trouble. Therefore we will not fear though the earth gives way, though the mountains be moved into the heart of the sea (Psalm 46:1-2).

In order for us to make it through our time of grief and find God's peace, we need to ask the Lord to help us shift our focus off of what we're feeling and onto His commands. The two commandments that are most important (and all-inclusive) are for us to love God and our neighbor (Matthew 22:37-39). Although at first you may have to just "gut it out," when you choose to worship the Lord and serve others out of a sense of duty, even though your heart is breaking, you'll soon discover that your sorrows will lessen and your problems will diminish by comparison. You'll discover that hope is growing again in your soul and that you can, even in the middle of your sorrow, sing songs of joy to Him. Below are some suggested ways for you to refocus your heart and fulfill the two great commands:

- Demonstrate a heart of love for God by specifically speaking to others about your trust of Him and belief in His faithfulness.

- Choose two or three hymns or gospel-centered choruses that feed your soul and magnify His goodness and commit them to memory. When you're tempted to give in to hopeless sorrow, begin to sing them by faith.

- Instead of hiding from and avoiding others, look for specific opportunities to serve. You might need to bring tissues along with you, in case your eyes start to flow with tears again, but be determined to love and minister to your neighbors in faithful obedience.

- Prayerfully consider how you might help a family member. Instead of retreating and licking your wounds, make your child his favorite dinner and tell him you still love him; go for a walk with your spouse and talk about the goodness of the Lord; take your other children out for an ice cream—not to talk with them about their wayward

sibling, but rather about their lives and to use the opportunity to tell them you love them.

- Memorize promises about God's willingness to answer
  prayer and recite them when you feel that your prayer is
  going nowhere. (See Question #1 at the end of the chapter
  for suggested verses to memorize.)

- Be very careful about how you speak about your wayward
  child to others who are not acting as your counselors. Your
  child's problems will grow, in your estimation, in direct
  relation to the amount of time you spend running him
  down. Instead, seek to cover his sin whenever you can, and
  speak to others about your trust in God.

- Remember that Satan is the one who is telling you that
  you'll always feel as badly as you do right now and that
  things will only get worse. Be assured that although your
  circumstance may not change right away, God will bring
  you relief as you seek to faithfully serve Him.

But, What If She...?

When our kids rebel, in addition to experiencing great sorrow,
we're prone to giving in to fear and worry. We start to wonder,
*What if he drops out of school? What if she gets sexually involved? Is
this a hopeless situation? Will he die on the streets? Is he cold? Is she
hungry? Who is preying on her now?* And perhaps our greatest
worry is for our child's soul: *What if he never turns to God and
dies under God's wrath? How could I ever be happy in heaven if one
of my children isn't there?*

The answer to these haunting fears is not blind optimism.
Well-meaning friends may assure you, "I know he'll come back
one day." But we don't know that. We don't know whether he'll

ever come back or even if we'll ever see her again. We should hope for the best, but the reality is that some rebels remain defiant. How will we ever rest again if we don't have solid ground to stand on?

The antidote to our worry is trust in God. In Matthew 6:25-34, Jesus commands His followers not to worry because their heavenly Father, who knows their needs, will take care of them. You can trust your Father to supply all your needs, both materially and spiritually, even in the midst of your difficult circumstance. Even now, when it seems to you that the Lord isn't being faithful to His word, you can rest in the truth that He's watching over you and supplying everything you truly need.

The fact God promises to care for us as a good Father doesn't mean that we'll live easy lives without any suffering. Though we can expect hardships, He promises that He won't place any trouble on us that we're unable to bear (by His grace). He's faithful to watch over and provide for us. And when we worry, we become guilty of disbelieving Him and His ability to care for us. That's what Jesus meant when He said that His worrying disciples were "of little faith" (Matthew 6:30). In the same way that we can find joy in sorrow, we can find peace in a storm by trusting in the veracity of God's word and in the faithfulness of His nature. *He's a good Father—this is your solid ground.* When it seems to you that your imaginations are more than you can bear, remember, He's a good Father. When you're tempted to let your mind wander down every dark alley, He'll be right there with you—He is a good Father.

Jesus knows our hearts. That's why He said, "Do not be anxious about tomorrow, for tomorrow will be anxious for itself. Sufficient for the day is its own trouble" (Matthew 6:34). He counsels you to control your anxious thoughts because you've got enough to handle being faithful today without worrying about what might happen tomorrow. In fact, His antidote for worry is to "seek first the kingdom of God and his righteousness" (Matthew 6:33). Instead of diverting time and energy into worrying about circumstances that are beyond our control, we should devote ourselves to serving God, and trusting that He knows and understands our concerns.

The Holy Spirit, through Paul, has lovingly given us these guidelines to overcoming our fears and worry:

> Do not be anxious about anything, but in everything by prayer and supplication with thanksgiving let your requests be made known to God. And the peace of God, which surpasses all understanding will guard your hearts and your minds in Christ Jesus (Philippians 4:6-7).

Although this passage is probably a familiar one to you, look closely at it again. What is your good Father telling you to do when you feel like you're drowning in a murky sea of worry?

He's telling you to express your trust in Him by praying about your concerns and being thankful. As you pray, feel free to bare your heart to God and cast your burdens upon Him. It will be important for you to fully yield all your worries, fading hopes, and shattered dreams to Him. Give them into His safekeeping and know that they are no longer your burden to carry. Much of our worry continues even after we pray because we still want to be in control. Join us in letting go, won't you? You know that you can't bear this burden alone, and you're wearing yourself out trying. Why not fully surrender your child's destiny to God, and entrust your child fully to His care?

You might pray something like this:

> *Father, I know that I've prayed about this many times before, but now I'm willing to give this situation fully*

over to You. Forgive me for my worry and for thinking that by my continued thought I would be able to change the course of my child's life. Forgive me for failing to trust in You and Your goodness and for thinking that my plan was better than Yours. I entrust my child to You now, and although I would pray that this cup of suffering would pass from me, I'm now willing to say with my Savior, "Not my will, but Yours be done." I submit myself to Your plan, even though I don't understand it, because I know You. You're a good Father. I also pray that You would help me get my eyes off of myself and my troubles and onto serving others and building Your kingdom. I trust You to give me the grace I need to make it through whatever may come. And Father, I'm most thankful for Your grace and kindness to me, and I know that You always hear my prayers. Thank You for Your faithfulness. Amen.

When we're in the midst of a crisis, it is easy to forget all of God's past and present goodness to us. That's why acknowledging our blessings can be a great cure for our worry. Often when the psalmist was in trouble, he would recall God's past faithfulness, which would give him hope and strength for the hour of difficulty. God has been good to us in the past, and we have every reason to hope for blessings in the future. Do you long for God's peace in your soul? The Lord will grant it to you as you entrust yourself, your child, and your future into His loving hands.[1]

The Price of Fear and Shame

Another concern you may have is a fear of what others think of you as a parent and the shame that you feel when you consider your child's choices. *How can I face the world when others discover that my son is a homosexual?* Or, *What will people say when they learn our daughter had an abortion?* Sometimes we feel as though we just can't stand the shame, the accusing looks, the insidious gossip.

While it's true that people sometimes do respond to our suffering in ungodly ways, we have to avoid fearing what others think, as Proverbs 29:25 says: "The fear of man lays a snare." If we're overly concerned about the opinions of others, we may fall into the trap of doing whatever it takes to protect our own reputation, rather than seeking what is best for the good of our family and the glory of God. We might avoid seeking help and counsel from church leaders because our status in the church may be threatened, or we may fear public embarrassment if our child is disciplined by the church. We may also find ourselves succumbing to a rebellious child's pressure and being tempted to change our standards to try to regain his approval. All of these are traps that can cause us to settle for people's approval rather than desire God's best for the situation.

Proverbs 29:25 concludes with the words, "But whoever trusts in the LORD is safe." When our chief concern is to honor and please God, we can trust the Lord to protect us. We can leave our reputation with Him and as long as He is pleased with us, it doesn't matter what others think or say. Though our sinful failures be many, He covers them by His mercy. He keeps us secure. When others criticize or judge us, we can remember that all of us stand only by God's grace. He's a good Father, and only His opinion matters—and not the opinions of others.

Dealing with Our Anger

We'll look at just one more emotion that's pretty common to all of us—that of anger. Most parents of wayward kids struggle with anger, and we may want to tell our child, "How could you be so ungrateful?" Or, "How could you hurt us in this way?" Sometimes our anger causes us to become sullen and shut down. "We established a pattern of sinful responses," one parent told us. "I would explode in anger and my husband would withdraw." That sounds pretty familiar, doesn't it? And sometimes our anger is not limited solely toward our child. We can become furious with anyone—including our spouse or our child's friends—who seem responsible for our current pain. We'll talk at length about anger in chapter 8, so for now, we'll share just a few quick thoughts you might find helpful.

We're Created in God's Image

Our capacity to experience anger and our sense of justice are part of what it means to be in God's image. God experiences and expresses anger, as Psalm 7:11 says: "God is a just judge, and God is angry with the wicked every day" (NKJV). We become angry when we believe we have been wronged, when we sense that the scales of justice are out of balance.

Our Anger Isn't Always Proper

Although anger is a natural response, that doesn't mean it is always proper. Because of indwelling sin, our anger often falls far short of God's righteous anger (Ephesians 4:26). Even though many parents claim theirs is a "righteous anger," we have to be very careful to not be deceived by sin's deceitfulness. Are we angry primarily because we are concerned about God's glory? Or because our child is acting in an offensive way toward such a good Father? Or is our anger characterized by unkindness, bitterness, and revenge?

We know that the truth about our anger is that it is rarely righteous. We're often more concerned about our own reputation and comfort than God's glory. Sometimes we're angry because we proudly believe that we deserve better than we're getting. *I've spent all this time and effort pouring into his life,* we may reason. *I've been a good parent, and this is how he repays me!* This may be hard to ask yourself right now, but is it possible that your anger flows from your desire to vindicate or approve of yourself? If so, you're not alone. Many of us find that our anger springs directly out of our proud, demanding hearts. *This isn't fair!* we think. *Our children should respect us!* We may even be tempted to become angry with God, an anger that is never justified, since God never does anything wrong.[2]

God Doesn't Express His Anger Against Us

Have you ever considered that God doesn't express His holy anger against us, His children, even when we demand our own way? Because He punished His Son in our place, He can justly forgive our sins (Romans 3:23-26) and He has no more wrath to pour out on us. If this is the way that our good Father has treated us, shouldn't we have the same loving, gracious attitude towards our children, even when they hurt us?

Consider the magnitude of God's gracious forgiveness in the Parable of the Two Servants in Matthew 18:23-35. You'll remember that one servant owed his master an unimaginable debt of ten thousand talents (the equivalent of 200,000 years' wages for a laborer), but when he pleaded for mercy, his master forgave him. A second servant owed the first servant a debt of seven hundred denarii (about 2 years' wages). When the second servant could not pay, the first was angry with him and treated him terribly. When the master found out about what the first servant had done, he "summoned him and said to him, 'You wicked servant! I forgave you all that debt because you pleaded with me. And should not you have had mercy on your fellow servant, as I had mercy on you?'" (verses 32-33).

It is significant that the amount owed by the second servant was no paltry sum. Anyone would be upset if someone cheated him out of two years' wages. We know that the hurt your child has caused you is also substantial. Yet all the wrongs our children have done to us are inconsequential when compared to our own sins against God and the grace He has shown us.

Live in the Shadow of the Cross

You'll find that you'll be able to overcome your anger when you spend time focusing on the magnitude of your debt before a good Father and the mercy you have experienced at His hand. Once you've come to terms with what the cross has to say about you (that you're so sinful you deserve to die, but so loved that Someone died in your place), you'll be better equipped to offer your child the same mercy and grace God has shown you.

My God, My God, Why Have You Forsaken Me?

Do you remember the verse at the beginning of this chapter? Let's go back to it, but this time, let's include the verse before it:

> My God, my God, why have you forsaken me? Why are you so far from saving me, from the words of my groaning? O my God, I cry by day, but you do not answer, and by night, but I find no rest. Yet you are holy, enthroned on the praises of Israel (Psalm 22:1-3).

Do you recognize this passage now? The beginning of it was uttered by your Savior as He hung on the cross, bearing the wrath of His Father for our sin and experiencing the terrifying judgment that was due to us. This is the picture that we want to leave with you.

We know that you feel alone, that you are suffering, and that you're being tempted to give in to the emotions that are raging in your tormented soul. We know the emotions: the shame, fear, excruciating sorrow, and anger that rends your heart in pieces. These emotions are very real...and we can either let them control us, or we can ask God to help us put them into proper perspective.

There is One who trembled with fear at what was approaching Him as He anguished in prayer in a garden, whose head was bowed in humiliation and grief as thorns pierced His holy brow, whose great and noble heart burst from sorrow, and who wondered, even if it was only for a moment, where His good Father was. This is your Savior, and this is the image you need to keep before you as you walk through this vale of tears He's calling you to. Remembering how He willingly suffered in your place can become the motivation you need to fight against your fears and worries and replace them with peace and holiness—for His sake, and for the sake of your family.

As C.S. Lewis' student said, "We read to know that we're not alone." We hope that after reading this chapter, you know that we're here with you, yet that's not what really matters, is it? What really matters is that the Suffering Servant has gone before you and is *with* you, right now as you read this book...and His grace and mercy will sustain you through this difficult season of your life.

Growing in Hope, Discovering His Help

1. Here are some verses well worth memorizing so that you
   can fight against the thought that prayer is useless and
   God doesn't hear you. Why not take time now to write
   them on index cards so you can keep them with you?
   Matthew 7:7-11; 21:22; Mark 11:24; John 15:7; Ephesians
   3:20-21; James 1:5; 5:16; 1 John 3:22; 5:14.

2. Read Matthew 6:25-33. How do these verses challenge you
   and comfort you? What do these verses reveal about your
   own heart and about your good Father?

3. As you consider the fears and angers you are experiencing,
   how much is taken up with the thought of others' opinions? Although it is difficult to be subjected to criticism
   and scrutiny, God can use these in our lives to free us from
   slavery to what others think and to grow in our Christ-
   likeness. Remember, He was criticized and shamed, too
   (see Galatians 1:10 and Psalm 56:4).

4. Sometimes we feel shame because we proudly assume that
   we deserve better and want others to think well of us. Is
   this the case with you? Ask the Lord to reveal your heart,
   and then respond to Him in faith.

5. Summarize this chapter in four or five sentences.

3

Your Divided House

No house divided against itself will stand . . .
—MATTHEW 12:25

Ｗe know that the pressures assailing you right now are daunting. You're facing great heartache, doubt, and fear as you watch your child—that sweet little cherub you loved to hug— turn into someone you never could have imagined. But that's not the only area of suffering for you, is it? Unless your wayward child is the only one living with you in your household, there are other people whose lives are being torn apart, too. It's normal for entire households to be thrown into turmoil when one child rebels. Families become divided against each other, with parents sometimes choosing up sides and siblings being torn between the two. More compliant siblings can end up being ignored, while others begin to behave in ungodly ways to test your love for them. Ultimately, everyone's life becomes focused on the one wayward child and the chaos he or she creates. One parent who has lived through this put it succinctly: "This situation has exacted a toll on all of our lives. The stress we endured during this time accounted for extreme emotional and physical ailments in our entire family."

Regrouping by Refining Your Focus

Are you nodding your head right now, saying, *Yes, that's us. Where did our peaceful little home go? Why is one child's rebellion ruining our whole house?* If you can relate to what we're describing, we have good news for you: This trial you're in won't last forever. We know that what you're going through is very difficult, but like all of our troubles here on earth, we can rest in the knowledge that one day, this trial will end. Perhaps it will end in your child's repentance and change—a hope that we all have. On the other hand, the chaos might lessen when you make the hard decision to send your child out of the home. Whether it ends very soon or after many more nights of trial and tears, you can be assured that *it will end.* In light of the temporal nature of this very distressing trial, let us encourage you to focus on the confession of your hope in God's faithfulness, and on caring for one another because the day (when all these trials *will* end) is drawing near:

> Let us hold fast the confession of our hope without wavering, for He who promised is faithful; and let us consider how to stimulate one another to love and good deeds, not forsaking our own assembling together, as is the habit of some, but encouraging one another; and all the more as you see the day drawing near (Hebrews 10:23-25 NASB).

Right now it's probably very easy for you to focus on the problems, lose hope, and attack one another. You may feel as though you're drowning in distress and may be wondering whether or not your faith will pass the test. The Lord lovingly tells us that the way to handle overwhelmingly tough times is to muse upon His faithfulness with a view toward encouraging each other. Take a moment now to think about the faithfulness of the Lord:

- How has He helped you in the past?

- Has He ever failed to strengthen you when you asked for help?

- Perhaps He hasn't delivered you from this present trial, but has He upheld you in it?

God's character never changes, and He declares that He is faithful (see 1 Corinthians 1:9). That means that He's dependable, reliable, and trustworthy. He's promised to be with you and help you in all your troubles and to keep you safe until He delivers you (Deuteronomy 31:6; Isaiah 41:10; Hebrews 13:5-6).

It's wonderful to be encouraged by the Lord, His nature, and His word, isn't it? And the encouragement He brings isn't merely for our own personal strengthening. The passage above from Hebrews tells us that we are to stimulate one another to good deeds, to gather together with other believers (and that would certainly include other believers in our own family), and to encourage each other. The problem, of course, is that we feel so drained and discouraged by the behavior of one (or more) of our children that the thought of getting together with one another for prayer, meditation on God's goodness, and mutual encouragement rarely enters our minds. Our trials may make us want to run and hide, but that isn't the Lord's counsel to us. Look again at the aforementioned bullet points. Did you answer the questions? (If you didn't, may we encourage you to do so now?) As you share these thoughts with your family, you might begin to see a change in your heart. You may see God's faithfulness more clearly, and you might become more aware of His peace as well.

Another way for you to stand firm in your faith through this trial is to continue fulfilling the top priorities in your life. Even though your concern for your child may be overwhelming, your marriage is still the most important relationship in your life—

and this trial, like no other, can easily divide you and your spouse unless you're very careful.

A Domestic Stress Test

The substance of your marriage is being tested right now, isn't it? We know that's possible because we've lived through the pressures you're facing. As biblical counselors and Christians who sincerely love and value God's Word, we assumed that our marriages could easily withstand any pressure. But now, our confidence has been refined. We've learned about the stress fractures that can surface in a marriage relationship, and how, in our trials, we need to rely on the Lord more than ever before.

Here's the obvious truth: It's not unusual for husbands and wives to disagree about how to handle a wayward teen. One usually tends to be more permissive while the other wants to be more strict. The permissive parent ordinarily sees the strict one as being strong in the area of justice, but weak at showing love and grace. The lenient parent may seem to excel at expressing love, but lacks the backbone to enforce standards. Then, as each parent reinforces their perspective of the other, they may over-react by becoming more strict or more lenient—in an effort to balance the other out. As one mother wrote, "Our differences in approach to discipline led to many arguments between my husband and I. In fact, by the time our son was a teenager, his problems had become a huge emotional drain on our marriage."

When a child's rebellion becomes evident, the situation can be further inflamed as a husband and wife blame each other for their child's sinful choices. "You drove him away by being so angry all the time!" a hurting mother may charge. "You let her get away with murder, so now she is completely out of control!" an angry and aching father may respond. As each parent feels threatened and unsettled by his or her child's behavior, the temptation for both is to point fingers at each other and shout, "This is all your fault!" When we say things like this, what we're really saying is, *If you had only been a better parent, I wouldn't be suffering like this!*

You can begin to change this dynamic of accusation and blame in your marriage by recognizing that this kind of speech is both harmful and unkind. In lobbing verbal grenades at each other, you're expressing anger, hurt, and bitterness in ways that displease the Lord while hurting the one person who can uniquely strengthen and support you during this heartrending time. You're also forgetting the Lord's direction to you to strengthen your spouse.

The next time you're tempted to lash out in pain at your partner, ask the Lord to help you remember Paul's admonition to the Ephesians: "Let no corrupting talk come out of your mouths, but only such as is good for building up, as fits the occasion, that it may give grace to those who hear" (4:29). Before you speak, ask yourself:

- Will my words build up my wife, who is suffering as deeply as I am?

- Will my words strengthen my husband and help him lead our family and learn of God's grace, or will it tear him down and discourage him?

Remember, *your spouse is not the enemy.*

Reaffirm and Refocus on Your Love

Sometimes the strain of dealing with a wayward child is so great that even though you stay together, your marriage will suffer from neglect and apathy. As you both become obsessed with the glaring problems of *that* child, you'll start to take each other for granted and you'll stop investing time and energy into each other's lives. You'll become exhausted and then irritable with each other.

Some grieving wives lose all sexual interest and may focus all their attention on the remaining compliant children or outside interests. Some hurting husbands withdraw emotionally or throw themselves into their work. Mixed together with the brew of accusation and conflict, this is a recipe for disaster, and even strong marriages can disintegrate before we're aware of what's happening.

What we have to remember is that this trial is distracting us from our main callings and duties. *God has designed marriage to be the primary human relationship,* a relationship that takes priority even over the relationships with our children (Genesis 2:24). When we honor God by focusing on our marriage and shoring up its foundation, it will remain strong and we'll be able to help our kids.

How long has it been since you went out with your spouse on a date night? When was the last time you had a conversation with your spouse that didn't center on your problems? How long has it been since you laughed together? Even though you are suffering, you can learn to enjoy and appreciate each other again. We know that your marriage can grow through this difficulty—it can be stronger, and the two of you can grow closer to each other and the Lord. Even though you're suffering you can know comfort through each other, as one mom said: "Even though my child doesn't seem to care about me, I am comforted by my husband's faithful love."

You'll be able to get your mind off of your own pain when you focus on ministering to your spouse's needs, emotions, and trials. Husband, what encouragement and appreciation can you offer to your wife today for being a dedicated mom and a delightful wife? Wife, how can you comfort your husband and help him to find relief from his troubles? Sometimes a back rub can be the most spiritual and soothing thing you can do for him. When we seek to live in ways that reflect our humble suffering Savior, who ministered to others even as He was afflicted, we'll find renewed joy and hope…and we'll rediscover the qualities that we loved about our spouse years ago, before the difficulties began. How long has it been since you looked into her eyes and said, "I love you, and I believe that we'll make it through this trial together"?

Although this is a terribly hard time for you both, many couples have told us that working together through the crisis of a wayward child has actually strengthened their marriage. One wife wrote, "I love and respect my husband all the more deeply for hanging in with me all those hard years.… Going through these years of trial together has firmly bonded us."

The First One to the Cross Wins

Sometimes when a dynamic of conflict and blaming is ongoing, we find ourselves competing against one another, trying to be the parent who stakes out the "moral high ground." For instance, making our child's disobedience all about our spouse's failures may make us feel better about ourselves. Of course, when this script is being played out, the acknowledgment of our personal failures, with the proper result of confession and repentance, fades from view. Let us challenge you to do something that we've tried to do as we've faced our family difficulties: strive to win the gospel race! Think to yourself: *If I'm the first to confess, the first to repent and humble myself, the first to the cross, I'll experience renewed grace from Him! I won't have to worry about trying to defend my own reputation or the "moral high ground." Instead, I'll be flooded with God's mercy.* Remembering that God resists the proud but gives grace to the humble (1 Peter 5:5) should motivate you to resist the temptations to blame, to hide, and to win.

In order to do this you'll need to take the Lord's admonition in Matthew 7:3-5 to heart:

> Why do you see the speck that is in your brother's eye,
> but do not notice the log that is in your own eye? Or
> how can you say to your brother, "Let me take the
> speck out of your eye," when there is the log in your
> own eye? You hypocrite, first take the log out of your
> own eye, and then you will see clearly to take the speck
> out of your brother's eye.

By the power of the Holy Spirit, examine yourself honestly.
Have you been playing the blame game instead of running the
gospel race? Have you been afraid to admit that some of the problems you're facing may have come from your own failures? If you
ask the Lord to show you your sins, He'll faithfully do so and you'll
be walking in the footsteps of King David, who said, "Search me,
O God, and know my heart! Try me and know my thoughts! And
see if there be any grievous way in me, and lead me in the way
everlasting!" (Psalm 139:23-24). If the Lord brings a matter to
your attention, go ahead and seek forgiveness from Him and your
spouse. You can seek forgiveness not only for your failures as a
parent, but also for the ways your careless words and unkind
actions towards your spouse may have made the current crisis
more painful for him or her. Remember, when you humble yourself, God will give you grace and strength.

One husband we know made great strides towards restoring
his family when he humbly admitted his faults as a parent and
sought his wife's forgiveness. He confessed that he had been lazy
and that he had failed to provide protection and oversight for his
children. He had neglected to consistently bring biblical instruction to his family, and would only react to glaring needs. He
sought forgiveness for being more concerned about pleasing his
son than pleasing God, and he committed himself to making
changes in the future. By doing this he did not lose his wife's
respect; rather, he became more worthy to receive honor from her.

He wasn't saying that she was without fault, but instead, his confession made it easier for her to get her mind off of his failures so she could deal honestly with her own sin. It's in ways like these (and many others) that God faithfully gives grace to the humble.

In the same way, a wife may confess that she's been too lenient with her children. Perhaps she has failed to recognize their sinfulness or was too gullible or easily deceived. Perhaps she stood between her children and her husband as he was seeking to administer discipline. Or maybe she cared too much about what others might think of her because of her children's outward appearance or earthly achievements, and failed to be focused on their hearts. In confessing these failures, she can count on God's grace to enable her to become her husband's helper rather than be a hindrance to his leadership.

Forgive One Another

If your spouse has confessed failures to you, let us encourage you to offer full and bountiful forgiveness. You won't be able to successfully sail around the dangerous shoals of familial disintegration if you're continually blown off course by the remembrance of one another's past failures. In love, you can promise not to bring up forgiven offenses and then seek to cover them over. Both Paul and Peter encourage us that love "does not take into account a wrong suffered" and it "covers a multitude of sins" (1 Corinthians 13:5 NASB; 1 Peter 4:8). This is the kind of love we need to begin to practice—the kind of love that God has for us in Christ.

We know that it will be very hard to forgive your spouse if you think that his sinful parenting has ruined your child. Please remember, however, that your child has made choices that he is responsible for, regardless of your spouse's inadequacies. Your child has freely chosen to respond to your spouse's sins by rebelling when, instead, he could have chosen to respond in humility and grace. The Bible teaches that none of us are unchangingly molded by influences in our environment, but rather, we respond with unique hearts to our unique circumstances. Your child's rebellion is not entirely your spouse's fault. Even though your spouse may have sinned against your child, and he is responsible for that sin, your child is also responsible for the way he's responding. Thinking in this way about your spouse's and others' failures will enable you to more freely forgive your spouse and more wisely deal with your wayward child.

As you consider how to forgive your spouse's sin (even if it's grievous), you'll need to remember the way that God has graciously forgiven you for your many sins, including your failures as a parent. It's very tempting to compare our sins to our spouse's and proudly refuse to forgive. Again, remember that God resists the proud, but gives grace to the humble. When we're being proud like this, we're forgetting the great debt that He's forgiven us for. We're forgetting how Christ suffered in our place, though He was sinless, and we're ignoring God's great and condescending love for us. In light of our Savior's sacrifice, we're commanded to fully forgive our spouse for past failures and trust God to help us show His unconditional love to one another. God's grace, which is poured out on the humble, can overcome past sins. If you are reading this book with your spouse, stop now and pray together. If you're reading it alone, find a time when you can share this portion of the book with him or her, humble yourselves and confess your sins to each other, and then drink deeply of your Savior's grace.

Work As a Team

Now that you've humbled yourselves before God and one another, you can recommit to working together through this crisis. This togetherness will be strengthened as you purpose to pray together daily. If you don't know how to do that, then just start by asking the Lord for His wisdom and asking Him to grant you both a renewed love for one another.

Accept and Rejoice in Your Differences

As you're growing in your unity, it's helpful for you to recognize that God has made you both different from each other for a reason. When Adam needed a companion, God didn't create another man like him. Rather, he made the woman as a suitable helper (Genesis 2:18). The husband and wife are designed to complement one another. Instead of trying to change your spouse to be more like you, seek to learn from each other's strengths. The very differences that have been dividing you (i.e., strict versus loving) can help you to form a united approach to your wayward child that balances both discipline and love. And because each of your children are different, one of you may be able to reach a certain child better than the other.

We will be able to take full advantage of our mutual strengths when we learn to respect our spouse and incorporate his or her perspective into our approach to dealing with our wayward child. When facing a challenge with your child, you can learn to say to yourself, *I don't want to draw any conclusions until I hear what my husband thinks because he often has understanding and perspective which I lack.*[1] This desire to hear your partner's perspective demonstrates a heart that's humble and teachable—a heart that God loves to pour His grace on.

Learn to Communicate in a God-Honoring Way

In order for us to grow into the team God intends us to be, we have to learn to communicate with one another biblically. When discussing a crisis, it's easy to focus more on being heard than listening to what our partner has to say. For example, you may have thought, *My husband is too strict (or tolerant) and I need to straighten him out.* Or, *I wish she would be quiet so I could tell her what she needs to hear!* Do these resonate with you? We know they do with us.

Rather than pressuring your spouse to let you have your say, James teaches that each of us should "be quick to hear, slow to speak, slow to anger" (1:19). Look again at the adverbs James uses: we're to be *quick* to hear, *slow* to speak and to anger. How would you rate your quick hearing and your slow speaking? Would your spouse say that you're slow to anger? These are difficult habits to put into practice, aren't they? Even though these steps we're recommending are difficult, we can trust that the Holy Spirit will enable us to grow and change as we rely on Him because our Lord has gone before us and assured our transformation.

In the same way that Christ humbled Himself, we should "do nothing from rivalry or conceit, but in humility count others more significant than yourselves. Let each of you look not only to his own interests, but also to the interests of others" (Philippians 2:3-4). How are you doing in looking out for your spouse's interests? Would your spouse say that you are humble, that you count him or her as more important than yourself? Are you more interested in hearing than being heard? In understanding than being understood? These are hard lessons for us to learn because we're so naturally centered on ourselves and our agenda. It's only as we seek to put on the character of Christ that we can learn the joys of humble servanthood and love.

Protecting Our Other Children

The next most important relationship after the one we enjoy with our spouse are those we have with our other children in the home. They, too, will be greatly affected by the crisis caused by their wayward sibling. They're aware that there is a spiritual battle going on at home, and they may feel caught in the crossfire and torn by loyalties to both sides. Their souls are also at risk, for the enemy would love to take them captive, too. Below you'll find some suggested steps you can take to protect your children from the war that's raging in your home.

Protect Them from Evil Influences

It is important to protect your other children from the sinful influences of your rebellious child. He may try to get his siblings on his side and may seek to influence them by boasting of his exploits or by exposing them to music, books, and videos that undermine your Christian beliefs and values (Proverbs 1:8-19; 1 Peter 4:4). If he's disrespectful, refuses to do chores, or participates in evil, your other children will notice and may be influenced to behave like him. He may try to undermine your authority by challenging the family's principles or by telling his brothers and sisters, "Dad's trying to brainwash you about Christianity. There is no ultimate truth. I'm finding my own beliefs and values, and I'm happy."

Should this happen, you will want to monitor—and if necessary, limit—the interaction between your rebel and his siblings. Please don't underestimate the spiritual risk to your other children. The Lord has called us to be shepherds in our families, and we must protect the little sheep from the wolves—in this case, from rebellious brothers or sisters (Matthew 18:6). You'll also need to protect your compliant children from other adults who side with the rebellious child, or who think that your parenting style is too strict.

Protect Your Other Children from Danger

Some wayward children are violent with their siblings. Others maliciously steal or destroy their property. As your family's shepherd, you must seek to defend them. If a child damages his brother's property, see that restitution is made. If he hurts or threatens his sibling, severe discipline must be imposed. Attacks upon siblings that put their physical safety at risk is grounds for removal from the home, as one father wrote: "Our son had taken years of humiliation and verbal abuse from his sister.... Our children are relieved that their sister is finally out of the house."

Don't Neglect Your Good Kids

It's easy to neglect our other children when we're devoting so much energy on the wayward child, isn't it? In light of this reality, it's important to make every effort to spend time with each of them, even if they don't seem to be having any significant problems. How long has it been since you played with them or scheduled fun family activities together? Sometimes you'll be forced to leave the rebel out because he can't or won't come, but don't let that stop you. Your children need to spend time with you away from the conflagration that's consuming their home.

It's easy to neglect discipline of the quieter kids in the same way that it's easy to neglect a little grass fire when a forest fire is raging out of control nearby. As we have learned from wildfires here in San Diego County, a little grass fire can easily turn into a massive blaze. So even as we're coping with a stubborn child, we have to be very intentional about maintaining the discipline, nurture, and instruction that God requires us to give to our "good" children.

Avoid Putting Your Other Children in the Middle

As parents of difficult children, we know that it's easy to be tempted to vent our anger, frustration, and bitterness on our other children. But they don't need to hear all the sordid details of their brother's escapades, nor should we pressure them to condemn their wayward sibling. Although sometimes we feel desperate for support and affirmation, we'll have to avoid leaning on our children to provide such, and instead, look to the Lord, who alone can provide the grace and strength we need.

Help Them Deal with Resentment and Bitterness

In the parable of the Prodigal Son, there was more than one child in the family. Remember what happened to the child who stayed at home, doing what his father desired? He was proud and became resentful about the grace that was shown to his prodigal brother. Listen to his speech when his brother was restored to the family:

> Look, these many years I have served you, and I never disobeyed your command, yet you never gave me a young goat, that I might celebrate with my friends. But when this son of yours came, who has devoured your property with prostitutes, you killed the fatted calf for him! (Luke 15:29-30).

Our faithful children may resent all of the attention being poured out upon their sibling: "You spent all this time and money trying to help him out, and all he does is waste your money and laugh at you!" she may protest. "You have all the time in the world to deal with her, but you can't even attend my play or soccer game!" Our kids will also be upset when they see what seems to be a double standard: "You punish me for one little slip-up and then let her get by with anything!"

As Christian parents, we've had to humble ourselves before our faithful children and seek their forgiveness for neglecting them, failing to protect them, having inconsistent standards of discipline, and foolishly wasting family resources. Do you believe you might need to do the same? If so, you could say, "Please forgive me for not paying enough attention to you over these past months. I should have been more available," and then ask the children to pray for you and your spouse. Then give your children the privilege of telling you when they feel they are being ignored. How often do you affirm your love and appreciation for the obedient children whose love brings you such joy?

Sometimes kids who are "good" can be tempted to become self-righteous and look down upon their disobedient sibling. If that happens, we need to gently remind them of their need for God's grace and forgiveness. As they model humble reliance on the Lord through confession of their own sin, they may be able to help win back their rebellious sibling. The whole family can pray for his restoration and anticipate the joy that will be yours when you celebrate Christ's forgiveness together (Ephesians 4:32).

See God's Goodness in Your Family's Time of Trial

Even though this is a very difficult time for you and your family, you can know with confidence that God is using it for your good. As you follow your Savior through this suffering, your faith will mature, your marriage will grow stronger, and your children will learn valuable life lessons about the foolishness of turning away from the Lord. As one father wrote, "For the siblings it was quite a lesson: the drama and pain that they witnessed have made a remarkable impact upon them to this day, and serve as an ever-present reminder of the need for purity and holiness before the Lord."

Although this is a terribly burdensome trial for you and your family, it can become a source of great strength and comfort as you see the changes the Lord is bringing about in your soul. Sometimes you may feel as if God has placed your soul in a vise that He is continuing to tighten and squeeze, making your life more and more uncomfortable. He isn't doing this because He loves to inflict pain or enjoys watching His children suffer. No, He's doing this because out of this painful pressure He'll distill the dew of a more refined faith, fervent love, and true humility—qualities that will bring you great joy and will feed and encourage those around you, too. You'll learn the great lesson of His Son and His faithful obedience in the midst of the winepress of God's wrath, and you'll come to love and appreciate Him all the more. Be encouraged, dear parent. You aren't alone in this trial and God has placed you here to support, protect, and inspire those whom He has placed in your life.

Growing in Hope, Discovering His Help

1. Read 1 Corinthians 1:9; 10:13; and 1 Thessalonians 5:24, and let the Lord speak to you about His faithfulness in your trial. Then read 2 Thessalonians 3:3: "The Lord is faithful, and He will strengthen and protect you from the evil one" (NASB). What do these verses mean to you today as you face these trials? Are you encouraged? Who can you encourage? For further study, you might also want to look up Hebrews 6:18.

2. What are your strengths as a parent? What are your spouse's strengths? Can you see God's wisdom in bringing you together? Share what you have written with your spouse.

3. What is your spouse's perspective on the problem of your wayward child? How does that differ from yours?

4. First Peter 5:5-7 says, "Clothe yourselves, all of you, with humility toward one another, for God opposes the proud but gives grace to the humble. Humble yourselves, therefore, under the mighty hand of God so that at the proper time he may exalt you, casting all your anxieties on him, because he cares for you." Ask the Lord to show you any areas of pride in your life that may be causing Him to oppose you. As He shows them to you, in humility confess your sin and ask Him for His grace. Cast all your worry upon Him, knowing that He will release you from this trial and exalt you in His time—and in the meantime, He will keep and sustain you.

5. As you look over the ways to protect your children (pages 62-66), can you see any areas in which you need to work? If so, enlist the help of your spouse and meet with your children, confessing sin when appropriate and asking for their input. Plan a fun outing together.

6. In four or five sentences, summarize what you learned in this chapter.

PART TWO

Understanding
the Ways of Your
Children

4

Fruit Inspection 101

Every good tree bears good fruit,
but the bad tree bears bad fruit.... So then, you
will know them by their fruits.
—MATTHEW 7:17,20

Have you ever noticed how the New Testament is filled with agricultural narratives? Fields and vineyards, sowing and harvesting, trees and their fruit filled our Savior's speech. That's because the land He traversed was packed with farmers and ranchers who would understand these word-pictures with ease. In this chapter, and the following one, we're going to refer to some of the Wonderful Counselor's word-pictures as we share how you can better discern your child's spiritual health.

Your New Occupation

Did you know that as parents we're called to be fruit inspectors? Are you surprised by that title? A fruit inspector is someone who closely examines pieces of fruit, checks them for wholeness, discerns whether they are the type of fruit they're represented to be, and determines their quality. Now, when we say that as a parent you're called to be a fruit inspector, we don't mean that you're to judge your child's motives or the inner workings of his heart. No parent can infallibly know their children's hearts, but we *can* evaluate the fruit that's growing in their lives, and from that draw conclusions about their heart. Since you've picked up this book (and stayed with us this long!), we're assuming that you're beginning to wonder if the kind of fruit you suspect might be growing from his heart is just a misshapen pear or if it is something more lethal, like a malignant hemlock. This chapter will suggest some practical ways for you to assess the quality of your child's walk before the Lord.

Perhaps you have recently begun to see some buds that look an awful lot like they might be hemlock. For example, he is less forthcoming and less respectful. Her friends are secretive and rebellious, and it seems as though they're purposely constructing barriers to keep you from seeing what's really going on. You're beginning to wonder, *Is this the normal process of tasty fruit maturation, or am I about to reap a deadly harvest of some poisonous plant?*

Don't Be Fooled by the First Bite

Jesus told a parable of two children whose lives might seem familiar:

> A man had two sons. And he went to the first and said, "Son, go and work in the vineyard today." And he answered, "I will not," but afterward he changed his mind and went. And he went to the other son and said the same. And he answered, "I go, sir," but did not go (Matthew 21:28-31).

As you read that, perhaps you thought, *I know those kids! Johnny seemed so compliant while Jane was so difficult. Now look at them—they've switched places!* Some children seem to come out of the womb bitter, strong-willed, and rebellious. From the time they begin to produce little buds, you know right away you're dealing with a wayward child. More than one mother has claimed to see the seeds of turmoil even when her children were very small. For this mother, the terrible twos become the tumultuous threes, and the struggle continued right through childhood into adolescence. And yet, by God's grace, this strong-willed child turned around and became compliant and loving.

Other children appear to be very compliant and loving from the beginning. They crave parental approval. We wonder, *Why can't all my kids be like her?* Yet as they grow older, the true nature of the fruit is known: the compliant, affectionate one becomes a rebel. They're like the second son in Jesus' parable, aren't they? They say whatever their parents want to hear, and then do what they want. Sometimes their rebellion builds gradually over time, as they decide that they aren't so interested in pleasing their parents and would rather please themselves or their friends. At other times, these children seem to take a sudden turn for the worse, frequently in connection with some outside influence like a boyfriend or a new crowd at school. We've even known kids who seemed to have successfully passed through adolescence only to turn away from the Lord during their twenties. What's going on here? Merely what the Lord said: You'll know them by their fruit, and *a bud doesn't ripen into mature fruit in one day.* Unlike the inspectors of fruit such as apples or oranges, we have to patiently test the fruit all along the way, helping our children to see the nature of what's really growing in their hearts.

This kind of fruit evaluation is a struggle for parents. It's hard because our kid's behavior changes from season to season, and we never know what to expect next. We realize that the thought of getting really involved in looking at your child's life may seem overwhelming to you right now. Perhaps you're so weary from the battle, just the thought of picking up another duty is staggering. Let us encourage you, however. The Lord isn't asking you to work out all your child's problems in one day. No, in fact, He's only asking you to be faithful for this day and not worry about the next. As we describe the ways you can watch for poisonous fruit in your child's life, don't despair if you suddenly discover some poisonous shoots. Remember that the Lord has both called and equipped you for this pursuit, and He'll strengthen you and help you to faithfully respond to Him and lean on His strength and wisdom.

Warning Signs to Watch For

In preparation for writing this book, we surveyed several families who have had significant struggles with their children. One of the questions we asked was, "How did the problem with your kids begin?" While some children expressed a strong will at a very early age, usually the crisis began sometime during the early teen years. As the parents reflected on their difficulties, they noticed several warning signs that were a precursor to further trouble. We've broken these signs down into two different categories: those that seem to develop from within the child, and the troubles that seem to originate from outside influences.

In this chapter, we'll examine the influences from *within*, and then in chapter 5, we'll look at the warning signs from without.

Influences from Within

Does he have a disrespectful attitude towards authority?

One of the primary tasks of parenting is to teach our children the proper response to God's authority, as this familiar command illustrates: "Honor your father and your mother, that your days may be long in the land that the LORD your God is giving you" (Exodus 20:12). This is primarily accomplished through the teaching of joyfully responsive submission to parental direction. We need to understand that although our children's obedience to us may not seem like such a big deal or even something we really think is necessary, we're not allowed to make that determination. Even when it's difficult and the battle seems to continue on endlessly, we're still required, *as those who are under God's authority*, to teach our children obedience, submission, and honor.

Does your child resent your telling him what to do? Has he become mouthy or more bold in his defiance of you or your spouse? Does she seem like she is seething all the time, occasionally indulging in outbursts of anger towards you or her siblings? Has he lost his job due to conflicts with his boss? Each of these manifestations (and others like them) involve a disintegration of respect for authority, something that the Lord will help you reestablish as you lean on Him.

Is he filled with discontent and ingratitude?

One of the easiest ways to assay the quality of fruit that's growing in your child's life is to listen to his speech. Would you say you are seeing some of what Paul described in 2 Timothy? "Understand this, that in the last days there will come times of difficulty. For people will be lovers of self, lovers of money, proud, arrogant, abusive, disobedient to their parents, *ungrateful*, unholy..." (2 Timothy 3:1-2, emphasis added). Is your child's speech filled with complaints, envious comparisons to other families, and discontentment and grumbling, even though you are making obvious sacrifices to provide for him? Although we all fight against the sin of discontent and complaining, these sins will be pronounced in the life of a youngster whose heart is bent in a certain direction and on living life according to his own plans.

Is he marked by laziness and lack of self-discipline?

Self-control or temperance is one of the fruits you will see growing in the life of a child who has the Holy Spirit (Galatians 5:23). Although we all have days when we feel more like lounging on the couch than mowing the lawn, a child who consistently shirks his responsibilities is displaying a fruit that is in opposition to the work of the Spirit in his life. Remember, there's more at stake as you consider his work ethic than whether or not you like the way he dusts his dresser, as this proverb tells: "He who gathers in summer is a prudent son, but he who sleeps in harvest is a son who brings shame" (Proverbs 10:5). What is at stake is the comprehension of his great need for Christ's saving power and then his submission to the work of the Holy Spirit in his life.

Here are some questions you can ask as you attempt to observe evidences of the Spirit's work (or lack of it) in your child's life: Has she lost all ambition to do well academically? Has he dropped out of sports, scouts, or musical activities? Does he just sit around and watch TV or surf the Internet all day?

Does the desire for secrecy mark her life?

One sure sign that there's bad fruit growing in your child's life is secrecy—the kind spoken of in Ephesians 5:12: "It is shameful even to speak of the things that they do in secret." Often parents wrongly assume that their child's demand for privacy is just a normal part of growing up. In one sense that's true, but in another sense it could be a danger sign. We aren't saying that you must monitor every little thing your child says or does, and we're not asking you to assume that there's something amiss if she likes to keep her bedroom door closed. We're just asking you to consider whether her behavior, in general, is becoming more reclusive and secretive. Is she refusing to give you information about her thoughts, her desires, and her activities? Does he just walk into the house and go straight to his room without saying anything? Does she resent your wanting to know where she's been, who she's been with, and what they have been doing? When he does emerge from his room, does he walk around with headphones on, isolated in his own world? One parent told us, "In a very short period of time he became aloof, reserved, sneaky, and secretive. Communication was superficial at best and was achieved only by persistent prying." Can you relate to this parent's experience? If you can, the Lord will sustain and bless you as you lovingly undertake more serious investigation.

Is he pursuing questionable intellectual interests?

Our children are being influenced by many different voices, and as they mature, the allure of these voices will grow louder and more persuasive. Paul warned the Colossians, "See to it that no one takes you captive by philosophy and empty deceit, according to human tradition, according to the elemental spirits of the world, and not according to Christ" (Colossians 2:8). Your children will hear teaching and philosophies that will oppose the truth you've taught them. They'll wonder what's wrong with Mormonism or Buddhism. Some youngsters begin to wonder whether there is such a thing as absolute truth, if there really is a difference between good and evil, or if your rules are merely an outgrowth of your "antiquated and narrow-minded" faith. Although an honest questioning of the faith you've taught them is proper and may be beneficial, there is also a great potential for our children to be harmed, particularly if they're being influenced by someone whom they perceive to be wiser or more understanding than their parents or pastors.

With that in mind, ask yourself these questions: Is he being unduly influenced by a particular teacher at school? Is he becoming overly interested in non-Christian religions and philosophies? Is he militating against your authority by taking a serious interest in Satanism, the occult, Eastern religions, or other distinctly non-Christian worldviews? Children who are gravely questioning or reacting against the faith of their parents will test them by resisting church attendance; then they'll fight against you and blame you for being oppressively restrictive of their freedom and self-expression (a phrase sometimes conveniently used to cover the desire to rebel or sin). It's during these times of trial that you'll need to stand against the onslaught of the devil through prayer, fasting, and consistent discipline. Remember, God has promised never to leave you and that He will give you strength in the midst of the battle as you put on the armor He's provided (Ephesians 6:11-18).

Have you gotten to the point of wondering if all your children's words are simply lying and deceit?

This last sign is probably the most pervasive in the heart of a child who is on the wrong path, because lying is at the heart of almost all rebellion. Many young people live a double life. They have learned to placate their parents through outward compliance—they know what their parents want to hear, they know what will keep them at a distance.

"Of course I'm committed to preserving my virginity. Why, I don't even want to date until I am ready for marriage!" she assures us. "Of course her parents will be with us the whole time; I wouldn't even want to be with her alone!" he protests. We, because we love our child, and also because we love the peaceful status quo, believe him or her. It's not that we shouldn't trust what they say; it's that we need to be wise and have an accurate picture of who they really are. If you've been seeing the aforementioned warning signs in your child, then you would be wise to begin to question your child's confident assurances. As one child who had been rebellious told us, "I was able to hide a lot of the bad things that I did, even though I think my parents knew about them. I was able to do this because I made sure there was no evidence they could find."

Even the child who refuses to learn at school can learn how to manipulate his parents and build trust as a ploy to get by with some forbidden activity. Many parents naively refuse to believe their children are capable of such duplicity. Of course, the truth is that our children can become master deceivers, as one parent wrote: "We appeared to receive outward compliance to the things we requested, but it became increasingly obvious that there was not an accompanying sincerity of heart." Like children dressing up on Halloween night, our children know how to disguise their rebellion and say whatever must be said in order to please and reassure our hearts. As parents, we've got to be wise; we've got to be willing to follow up when we suspect lies or duplicity, even if that means that our child will be angry with us. We've got to consistently remind them that we must not "lie to one another, seeing that you have put off the old self with its practices" (Colossians 3:9).

Don't Panic, the Crop May Not Be Ruined!

Please don't conclude that because you've seen one or more of these warning signs that your child is lost to you. As children enter into adolescence and young adulthood, it is very normal for them to strive to establish their own identity, and to question the identity they have received from you. It is normal for a teenager to be influenced by his peers. And because their bodies are growing and changing, most teens are beset by laziness, and even the best kids can be moody and mouthy from time to time. But the mere fact that these things are normal does not change the truth that they are wrong, and if they persist, you may need to be more wary.

If you've resonated with some of these symptoms, we've got work for you to do now. But first, don't give up hope—perhaps the Lord has brought you to this place and placed this book in your hands so that you can be the means of rescue that your child needs before it's too late.

If you have recognized some of these warning signs in your child's life, the Lord is calling you to seriously pursue your calling as a fruit inspector. Because rebellious children can be very secretive and deceitful, you'll have to look beyond what they allow you to see of their lives. Their secretiveness will make it harder for you to examine them. Don't panic or despair or think that your child is worse than anybody else's. We all seek to cover our sin, just like Adam did in the Garden of Eden, but God lovingly called him out and exposed his shame, for Adam's benefit and change.

Your Child's Spiritual Condition May Surprise You

Many young adults who have been brought up in Christian homes ultimately question their faith, wondering if they are Christians because Christianity is true or if they're Christians simply by familial default. They realize there is a whole world full of people who sincerely hold to other beliefs. They may see some of these people as nice and intelligent, and this may cause them to question whether Christianity is absolute truth. *Don't be shocked when this happens to your child.* Salvation must be affirmed in each individual's own heart, and isn't transferred merely through family ties. Such questioning may turn out to be a blessing to your child because it may ultimately result in a healthy reaffirmation of the gospel.

Understand that while you can control behavior through discipline, you can't control what your child believes. When one of my sons began to question the truth of Christianity, he was very fearful because he assumed that since I am in Christian ministry and my faith is paramount to me, I would impose very harsh punishments for his failure to believe in the truth that I hold so dear. My relationship with him greatly improved when I admitted to myself and to him that I couldn't force him to believe as I do. I began to understand that he needed to choose his own religion and lifestyle and that in order to have an ongoing relationship with him, one in which he felt free and safe to express his personal beliefs, or to question mine, I would have to assure him that he could do so without fear of my reprisal. I now see my role with him as an evangelist, seeking to persuade him of the glories of the gospel of Christ. I recognize that I cannot compel his faith, but can only point him to the Savior I love and serve him as an involved and active father.

I also had to explain to him that while he is free to believe in his heart that Buddhism is true, or that marriage is an unnecessary social convenience, like me, he is still accountable to God for his beliefs and actions. So long as he lives in my home he must live, at least externally, according to biblical moral norms, and must attend church with the family—if not to worship, then to be exposed to God's Word so that he can make his own choice. This is the heartbreaking road that I've had to walk with him, but it is a road on which my wife and I experience the grace and pleasure of the Lord. Although at this writing we're still waiting to see true repentance and faith in him, our relationship as father and son has grown immeasurably, and my wife and I are still believing that he'll turn towards the Lord and refresh our hearts once again.

—Jim

In the course of reading this chapter, were you shocked or concerned at the number of ways that you've seen your child being described? We can imagine that these revelations may have come as an unwelcome and disconcerting foreshadowing of problems to come. Please don't let this cause you to put this book down and try to hide from what may be transpiring in your home. It certainly does seem easier to just ignore problems instead of tackling them and trying to root them out, doesn't it? We know that because we've been there and we've had to fight the same fight you're fighting right now. Let us encourage you by saying that the most important step you can take right now is to meditate on the Lord and His love for you and your children like you never have before.

Growing in Hope, Discovering His Help

1. Read Matthew 7:16-29, 2 Peter 2:10-18, and Jude 1-13. What do these passages teach you about the relationship between the true nature of a tree and its fruit? What do they say about people who pretend to be believers but aren't? What do they say to you about your children?

2. Write a list of all the questions you answered *yes* to (pages 74-78). Ask your spouse or a trusted family friend if he or she agrees with your assessment. Begin to pray specifically about each of these items.

3. Does your child exhibit a disrespectful attitude toward authority? Read Exodus 20:12, Romans 13:1-2, and Proverbs 24:30-34. What is God's perspective on authority?

Why is it important for your child to learn to subject himself to authority—is it just a matter of his obeying you, or is there something more at stake? If so, what might that be?

4. Does it seem to you that your child is discontented and ungrateful? How do these characteristics manifest themselves in your child's life? What do you think that this means about the true nature of his heart?

5. Is your child lazy? Does he lack self-discipline? Here's how Paul described the Christian life:

> Do you not know that those who run in a race all run, but only one receives the prize? Run in such a way that you may win. Everyone who competes in the games exercises selfcontrol in all things. They then do it to receive a perishable wreath, but we an imperishable. Therefore I run in such a way, as not without aim; I box in such a way, as not beating the air; but I discipline my body and make it my slave, so that, after I have preached to others, I myself will not be disqualified (1 Corinthians 9:24-27 NASB).

Is your child's life characterized by a focused self-discipline for the sake of the gospel? Although we all have ups and downs, what does the focus of your child's life tell you?

6. Is your child becoming increasingly more secretive? Usually children want to hide what they're doing because they are ashamed or because they want to avoid your censure. What do you know about her life, her friends, her goals, and interests? Does he welcome you in or try to shut you out? These are the questions you'll need to consider as you seek to gain an accurate perspective on your child's life.

7. In four or five sentences, summarize what you've learned in this chapter.

5

Fruit Inspection 102

God said, "Let the earth sprout vegetation…
fruit trees on the earth bearing fruit after
their kind"…and it was so.
—Genesis 1:11 NASB

A t the dawn of creation, God set a principle into motion that has never changed: Every tree bears fruit "after its kind." Apple trees always bear apples, and orange trees always produce oranges. That's just the way it is. In this chapter we're going to continue to help you discern what kind of fruit is growing from your child's life. This inspection will enable you to determine if you're dealing with a good apple tree that's just produced some sour apples (which does happen), or if you're dealing with a different sort of tree that is producing what Jesus would call "bad" fruit (Matthew 7:17).

Please believe us when we say that you needn't despair for your child! Although the principle of producing fruit "after its kind" has never changed, the God who created all trees and all of our hearts can and does change our very natures, causing us to become people who can bear good fruit for His glory. Just as an orange tree can't turn itself into an apple tree, none of us can change our own natures, but we needn't despair. There is always hope that the Lord will do what none of us can do for ourselves. God is the heart changer, as Ezekiel wrote:

> I will sprinkle clean water on you, and you shall be clean from all your uncleannesses, and from all your idols I will cleanse you. And I will give you a new heart, and a new spirit I will put within you. And I will remove the heart of stone from your flesh and give you a heart of flesh. And I will put My Spirit within you, and cause you to walk in my statutes and be careful to obey my rules (36:25-27).

God can cleanse your children; He can give them a new heart and a new spirit. He can remove their stony heart and give them a warm heart of flesh; and He can put His Spirit within them and cause them to love and obey His law. What great hope we can have! Even if after you inspect the fruit that your kids are growing you conclude that they aren't really His, God can change them! Why not take time right now to ask the Lord to reveal your child's true nature to you? Ask Him to give you the courage to honestly assess him and his fruit and then to change him into a luxurious fruit tree loaded with a luscious, juicy crop.

Warning Signs to Watch For

In the last chapter we looked at warning signs that flow primarily from within, now we'll examine warning signs that are marked by influences from the outside.

Influences from Without

Is he continually choosing the wrong kinds of friends and too dependent on his peers' approval?

"Do not be deceived: Bad company ruins good morals" (1 Corinthians 15:33). Wicked friends will have a significant influence on your child's outward behavior. The nature of friendship is one of sharing commonalities and intimate bonding. Our kids befriend people who provide what they want: a sense of acceptance, a desire for freedom or excitement. Our children's very choice of friends tells you a lot about the nature of their hearts. Do they choose godly, wise children, or do they scoff at "goodie-goodies" and desire the approval of unbelievers?

Perhaps in the past your child has habitually followed your lead, desiring peace with you and pleasing you rather than following after questionable friendships. Then he met *that* girl, and he seemed to change overnight. It is important for you to realize that the mere fact that he's drawn to an unbelieving, ungodly girl reveals the real fruit that's secretly growing in his heart. You might not have seen this before because the girl happened to be the catalyst that helped to reveal his true nature.

As you begin to assess the kinds of friends your children embrace, here are some questions you can ask: Do I know my children's friends? Is my child's peer group becoming a stronger influence in his life than the family? Do I like my children's friends? Do my children's friends seem to like me? Do I find that while I can't get five words out of her, she spends hours talking on the phone, or chatting on the Internet? Is he changing his appearance to please his peers? Am I battling my daughter over the appropriateness of her clothes?

Is she sustaining an inappropriate relationship with the opposite sex?

Relationships with the opposite sex are particularly significant because they appeal to our youngsters on so many levels—which is why Paul wrote this earnest warning: "Flee youthful passions and pursue righteousness, faith, love, and peace, along with those who call on the Lord from a pure heart" (2 Timothy 2:22).

Why does holding onto a certain boyfriend mean more to your daughter than the concern of possibly falling into an impure sexual relationship? It declares to all her friends that she's a woman, she's no longer a baby, she has value, she's desirable, she can hang out with the really cool kids because *he's* interested in her. Likewise, young men often measure their value as men by what kind of girl they can get. He'll think that he's *really* a man if he can get *that girl* involved with him. And if she's interested in him sexually, that makes him feel like he's strong and virile and measures up to all the stereotypes of what it means to be a successful man in our society. Then, of course, there is the bodily pleasure that accompanies sexual sin—a pleasure that may compel a young man to throw off the restraint that he's been taught.

Many young people become involved in serious relationships that are like "mini-marriages" and often lead to broken hearts, sexual immorality, and disrupted family relationships. Don't underestimate the influence romantic attraction can have on your teen. A mother once told a man in our church that her college-aged son was reconsidering the teachings of Christianity. His wise question was, "Who is she?" He guessed right.

As you consider the gravity of your child's relationship with the opposite sex, you might ask yourself: Is my child bonding with someone whose approval and love means more to him or her than the Lord's? Does this person love God and encourage my child to love Him, or is this person simply interested in fulfilling his physical and emotional desires through my child? The desire for romance and sex can easily pull a child away from his family's influence and protection, and can quickly have the wrong kind of influence on your child's heart.

Is he delighting in objectionable entertainment?

Our culture is riddled with filthiness, immorality, impurity, and crude joking. As was made so evident in a recent Super Bowl halftime show, we can't even watch sports without being assaulted by perversion, covetousness, and impurity. As bad as that show was, it was simply a mild form of the kind of sludge that's pumped out daily through all forms of music, movies, magazines, and the Internet. These influences don't just entertain, they are intentionally meant to tear down the walls of protection and wisdom you've sought to raise. They appeal to young people's lust and desire for independence from authority. "But sexual immorality and all impurity or covetousness must not even be named among you, as is proper among saints. Let there be no filthiness nor foolish talk nor crude joking, which are out of place, but instead let there be thanksgiving" (Ephesians 5:3-4).

Is he listening to music that expresses angst, anger, and rebellion? Is she attracted to movies that glorify immorality and impurity, unkindness and worldliness? Does he seem to find delight in that which is crude and objectionable? Is she laughing at shows that mock your standards and your Savior?

Is he experimenting with forbidden substances?

In the same way that sexual immorality appeals to and entices not only the mind and emotions of our children, but also their physical bodies, substances such as nicotine, alcohol, marijuana, and harder drugs appeal to their sinful desire to be autonomous.

At the same time, these substances produce a pleasurable sensation that numbs our children's consciences and creates an ever-stronger desire for more. Our children can become entrapped like Edmund, C. S. Lewis's character in *The Lion, the Witch and the Wardrobe,* whose desire for the enchanted Turkish Delight would never be satisfied by another bite of it—"…anyone who had tasted it would want more and more of it, and would even, if they were allowed, go on eating it till they killed themselves."[1] Kids often express their growing rebellion by experimenting with cigarettes, and then graduate on to alcohol, pot, and harder drugs. Do you smell smoke on his clothes? Does he tell you it was from someone else? Are there any signs of drug use or drinking, such as slurred speech or red and glazed-over eyes? Have you noticed a decrease in his appetite or a change in her sleep patterns? Does she claim that her friends smoke, drink, and do drugs, but that she is trying to be a good influence on them?

As parents, we're sometimes unwilling to face the terrifying possibility that our children may be entrapped by such harmful and dangerous substances, and so we're tempted to bury our heads in the sand. We ignore the warning signs that God has lovingly posted in our path as we naively insist, "Not my child! He always promised that he would never use drugs!" Some parents learn all too late that their child has already been drinking or using drugs, and doing so for years. Looking back, they admit to suspecting that something was wrong, but they didn't want to deal with it. Asking the aforementioned questions may seem overly suspicious or unloving, but doing so is a sign that you're willing to do the hard work, that you love your child more than you love yourself, that you value his eternal soul more than your reputation as a "good" parent, and that you desire true peace instead of an ungodly truce. It is this kind of parent who tells the child, "You were bought with a price. So glorify God in your body" (1 Corinthians 6:20).

Don't Be Mistaken About Your Child's "Rights"

One myth our culture propagates is that teenagers deserve an absolute right to privacy, but that's not the biblical or loving perspective. God has put our children under our care, and we're accountable to Him to protect them from evil. While only God is all knowing, we need to try to learn whether our children are abusing substances, being sexually immoral, or engaging in illegal activities. Please don't underestimate the number of lies they may tell in order to keep you off of their backs or out of their business. If trust is breaking down, don't assume they are telling you the truth about where they are going, who they're talking to on the phone, or what they are doing on the Internet. Be wise, look closely, and ask the Lord to help you really see, as Ephesians 5:11 says: "Take no part in the unfruitful works of darkness, but instead expose them."

As you begin to really investigate your children's fruit, you'll need to make it clear to them that so long as they are minors living in your home,[2] you have the obligation *under the Lord* to gather information about their lives. If you have reason to suspect wrong activity, you may find it necessary to search their rooms and backpacks, check up on their claims to be somewhere, monitor their phone conversations, email, Internet chats and Web sites, and if necessary, test them for drug and alcohol use.

If this is the case, your child, who's undoubtedly bought into the world's perspective of her right to privacy, will react with fury and incredulity. She may cry, "You don't trust me!" to which you may reply, "I am giving you an opportunity to earn my trust." He may tell you that you don't have any right to go through his things because he owns them. Again, you'll need to stand firm, loving him more than you need his approval, and informing him that you're responding to the Lord, who has given him into your care.[3] Remember, when God approached Adam about his sin, Adam's first response was to hide and then blame someone else. Your child will probably do the same thing. God, in His love and grace, persisted with Adam, and so must you persist with your child.

Inspecting Fruit Is Hard Work

As you begin to look closely into your child's life, you'll come to discover that inspecting their fruit is hard work. You'll need to spend time and effort getting to know your children's friends and their parents. You'll need to understand the cultural influences on your child such as the music he loves and the movies she sees.[4] Why not watch her favorite films with her and then talk about them afterwards? If your child has access to a computer, you'll need to purchase Internet monitoring software,[5] all the while recognizing that many of our kids know more about computers than we do.[6] You may even have to go to the trouble and expense of purchasing and administering drug or alcohol tests. It's probably becoming obvious to you now that you may have some catching up to do. You might also need to get someone else to help. Please don't delay in pursuing your child, especially if he's hiding from you.

We admit that as parents we often fail to keep our kids safe because we are not willing to sacrifice the time, the effort, or the money to adequately keep up with them. It's very tempting for us to look the other way, especially if our children seem to be conforming externally. And perhaps deep down, we fear what we might find if we were to look beyond the surface of our child's life, and we don't want to face this reality. We're comfortable with the status quo (even if it isn't that great!), and we hope perhaps our kids will eventually change for the better. In doing so, we sometimes maintain the illusion of peace where there are problems. We know these things because we're just like you, but by faith we're seeking to heed the warnings of Old Testament prophets such as Jeremiah and Ezekiel. Jeremiah wrote, "They have healed the wound of my people lightly, saying, 'Peace, peace,' when there is no peace" (6:14). Do you avoid the hard work and pain of stitching up a gaping and infected wound by covering it with a Band-Aid? Do you *just want some peace* when in reality there is no peace?

Ezekiel was in a similar circumstance. He knew that if he warned God's people about their wrong behavior and God's impending judgment, they would hate him. But the Lord instructed him that if he failed to warn them, God Himself would punish him (Ezekiel 33:5-6). Yes, we're between a rock and a hard place, aren't we? If we fail to warn our children, God may discipline us; but if we warn them, they might respond in anger and hostility. When we frame the choices in this light, the road that we must take is obvious. While we are not accountable for every choice our children make, we will answer to the Lord for how diligently we obeyed Him and kept watch over the young ones He entrusted to us.

In another picture from Ezekiel (chapter 34), God condemned the selfish, lazy shepherds in Israel who didn't watch over and protect His people. Imagine your child as a sheep who has wandered into the woods, out of your sight. You can choose to focus on your own busy life, or you can drop everything and rush into the woods to rescue your child from danger before the wolves get her. One parent wrote, "We were naive and were thinking his friends were a better influence than they turned out to be. In retrospect, we should have tried to keep a closer eye on him and the friends he spent time with." Another parent lamented, "We were being 'shined-on'...I wish that I had been more discerning earlier. I wish I had taken more time to...observe in more detail the different activities and priorities in my child's life."

Braving the Discovery of Your Child's True Heart

In the same way that a tree won't be able to consistently produce delightfully satisfying fruit if it isn't, in fact, a fruit tree, your child won't be able to conform to the beliefs and practices of Christianity if he isn't really converted. One of the biggest mistakes we can make is to assume that our rebellious children are believers. A mother of a drug dealer may object, "But I remember when she was five years old and she prayed by her bed to invite Jesus into her heart." A father may remember his son's public confession of faith through baptism when he was eleven.[7] But do these prayers and confessions of faith guarantee that our child's faith is real?

The Bible teaches that even among adults, not every profession of faith is real. In the parable of the soils (Mark 4:1-20), the seed that fell on the rocky soil and among the thorns, after initially sprouting, died without bearing fruit. Some kids who make a profession of faith when they're little turn away when the persecution of peer pressure begins (Mark 4:16-17). Some kids who claimed to trust Jesus at an early age choose to love the world and turn their backs on Christ (Mark 4:18-19). In fact, the Lord warned that in the time of His judgment, even some who call Him their "Lord" will be shown to have never been truly converted (Matthew 7:21-23).

How should we respond as parents when our child makes a profession of faith? We should encourage and commend him or her. But we should also realize that, just like the seeds in the soil in Jesus' parable, only time will tell whether the conversion is genuine. Some children may make a profession of faith in order to please us, to be accepted by the church community, or because that is what their friends are doing. We know of several young people who admit that their youthful baptism or other public expression of faith was motivated by their desire to please men rather than God. Others, who are now walking with the Lord, look upon their period of rebellion as a temporary time of backsliding.

How can you know whether your child's profession of faith is genuine or not? As we've said all along, Jesus taught that a person's true nature can be known by the fruit of his life. Remember, consistently sinful actions spring out of a corrupt, unbelieving heart. It's not that believers are incapable of great sin, for that does happen at times. It's just that great folly can't be part of their consistent lifestyle.

The Tests of Spiritual Life

Anticipating the trouble we would have in our attempts to discern those who are really Christians, the Holy Spirit inspired John to write the entire book of 1 John so that we "may know" we have eternal life (1 John 5:13). Rather than merely asserting that anyone who asks Jesus into their heart is saved, John gives us three tests of spiritual life. These same tests can help you discern whether your child is really a believer or not.

A Heartfelt Confession

Those who have eternal life believe and confess that Jesus is the Christ. "Whoever confesses that Jesus is the Son of God, God abides in him, and he in God" (1 John 4:15). The confession of which John speaks is not merely an external verbal mouthing of words. The demons believe in God and know who Jesus is (James 2:19; see also Mark 1:24). A true confession springs from a loyal heart and expresses itself consistently in every aspect of a believer's life and relationships. Does she profess Christ when at school? Is he unashamed to be called a Christian around his friends and the people on his baseball team?

A Genuine Obedience

Those who truly know God obey His commandments. "By this we know that we have come to know him, if we keep his commandments. Whoever says 'I know Him' but does not keep his commandments is a liar, and the truth is not in him" (1 John 2:3-4; see also John 14:15).

This verse doesn't mean that a true Christian perfectly keeps all of God's law (see 1 John 1:8-10 and 2:1). What it does teach is that when God saves someone, that person receives the Holy Spirit and a new nature (2 Corinthians 5:17), and the Holy Spirit inevitably produces good fruit (Galatians 5:22-23). The person who consistently and shamelessly practices lying, stealing, or sexual immorality is showing that his life is devoid of the Spirit. John calls a person—someone who claims to be a Christian but habitually disobeys God's commandments—a liar. The Bible tells us that a child like this remains unconverted, no matter what he says about himself.

A Love for Fellow Believers

Those who truly know God love God's people. "Whoever loves his brother abides in the light, and in him there is no cause for stumbling. But whoever hates his brother is in the darkness and walks in the darkness..." (1 John 2:10-11). If your teen's life is centered around his own non-Christian friends and if he looks down upon other believing kids as hypocrites or "goodie-goodies," then he is probably not born of God. Does your child love to be around those who love God?

The Great Hope in Knowing the Truth

Facing the hard reality about your child's spiritual condition should change your focus and give you hope. If the fruit of his life shows you that his heart is far from God, your efforts and your prayers should be towards his conversion, not a mere change in his outward behavior. If he claims to be a believer, you can appeal to him, pointing out that his life doesn't match his profession of faith. Your focus can be on communicating the transforming grace of a genuine relationship with the Lord, and in doing so, your hope can be that if God truly gets hold of his life, the change will be dramatic and joyous.

Another benefit of accurately evaluating your child's spiritual condition is that there are differences between what you can expect from a converted child, as opposed to what to expect from one who hasn't tasted grace yet. For example, while it's important for all children living in the home to respectfully attend Sunday worship times and family devotions, you may allow your unbelieving teen to choose for himself whether he wants to sing or to pray out loud. You may also allow him to make some choices about whether or not he will attend extra church activities.

It's hopeful to tell an unconverted child that he may not really be the Lord's because what he's experienced of Christianity is just a dim shadow of the true joys found at the cross. It will give him hope to know that there's something more than what he's experienced, and that the Lord really can transform his life.

We've each counseled young adults who were raised in Christian homes and who had made professions of faith during childhood, but during their teen years got involved, usually secretly, with sin. These kids went to church out of duty and were bored. But then God, by His great power and grace, truly worked in their lives, and they began to deal honestly with their parents and the Lord. They started battling their sins and sought biblical counsel and accountability. They began taking an interest in attending church and in personal Bible reading and prayer. We are convinced that in many of these cases, these young people had just become believers, and even though they may have intellectually accepted some of the facts of the gospel at an earlier age, God had only recently granted them heart repentance and faith. The result was a life dramatically changed by the power of the Holy Spirit: "If anyone is in Christ, he is a new creation. The old has passed away; behold, the new has come" (2 Corinthians 5:17).

As a parent, this is your hope: *the new can come, even for your child!* Although you may be experiencing sorrow and deep concern now, especially as you've read over this chapter, God's power is great and His steadfast love is strong. Remember that He can change even the hardest heart of stone into a warm, gentle heart of flesh. He delights in particularly hard cases—the base, foolish, and most wicked ones—fashioning them into trophies of His grace. For example, Paul was murdering Christians when God stepped in and transformed his life. Don't despair, dear parent. God is able to change your child's heart and cause him to love His Son. Your call is to remain faithful and consistent, facing the hard road ahead with trust in the God who sees your child as he really is and can change him for His glory.

Growing in Hope, Discovering His Help

1. What do 1 Corinthians 15:33, 2 Corinthians 6:14, and Proverbs 13:20 teach about friendships with the wrong kind of people? What do you know about your child's friends? What can you do to find out what you need to know about them?

2. According to Genesis 2:24, marriage is the right time for a romantic commitment: "For this reason a man shall leave his father and his mother, and be joined to his wife; and they shall become one flesh" (NASB). Have you given in to the pressures of the world and your child and allowed him or her to become involved in sexual sin or unsuitable romantic relationships? What will you do to regain the ground that's been lost? (This is where help from a pastor or mature Christian will be invaluable. Ask this person to pray, to hold you accountable, and to guide you when you're wavering in the battle.)

3. Read 1 Corinthians 6:20 and Proverbs 20:1, and 23:29-30,33. What do these verses teach you about the improper use of substances and the proper care of our bodies? If you believe that your child is involved in substance abuse,

please get help from your pastor, a wise Christian friend, or a biblical counselor without delay. Also, in Appendix B, we've furnished you with information about organizations that can help you if you think your child has a problem with substance abuse. Be aware that it will be very difficult for your child to stop once he's begun, because addictions affect both the mind and the body.

4. What are the three tests of true faith that the apostle John gave us? How do you measure up to those tests? If, as you read them, you're seriously wondering whether you measure up, don't despair! Perhaps the Lord has let your relationship with your kids get to this point to show you that you may not really be His. For more on this, please turn right away to Appendix A. On the other hand, if you're assured of your salvation, how does your child measure up to the three tests? How does being able to discern his or her real state help you and give you hope? (And, if you're wondering whether or not your child can lose his salvation, please read endnote number 8 on page 251.[8]

5. In three or four sentences, summarize what you've learned in this chapter.

6

But My Child Is Different!

Dr. Laura Hendrickson

*...so that the works of God might
be displayed in him...*
—John 9:3

⌒⌒⌒

If your child is among those who have special problems, you may have started wondering by now whether this book applies to your situation. For example, your child may have been diagnosed with a learning disability. You may have been told your child suffers from ADHD, bipolar disorder, or Tourette's syndrome. He may even have been diagnosed with a developmental challenge such as mental retardation or autism. Maybe you have had the heartbreak of being told that your child is schizophrenic. How do you respond in a godly way to a child who is rebellious yet also has special problems? This chapter will address a general approach to challenged kids, and the following one will offer more specific help for your child's particular challenge.

A Challenged Child Has Unique Problems

In one sense there is nothing in this book that does not apply equally to your child, in spite of his challenges. And yet your situation is different, too. Your child may have medical problems, and may be taking psychiatric medicines. He may have school problems that affect his learning, his behavior, or both. He may experience serious difficulties in his relationships with other kids because of his problem.

Your child may have been placed into special education classes, which have set him apart from his peers and made him uncomfortably aware of being different. Classmates can be cruel to a "special ed" child because the label makes him stand out in a kid culture that values conformity above all else. His behavior in the classroom (or his physical or social clumsiness) may make him stand out even if he hasn't been formally labeled. As a result, his experience is often what teacher Rick LaVoie calls, "the last one picked and the first one picked on."[1]

Every child responds in a different way to pressures like these. Some may keep trying to please their peers and teachers. But giving up is a more common response. If he has difficulty with his studies, he may stop trying to do well and begin misbehaving in class instead. If he has difficulty holding his own in social situations, he may blow up frequently with physical or verbal aggression in response to conflict with his peers.

You may also struggle to respond in a godly way. You may find yourself in the uncomfortable position of needing to enforce the school's standards for your child's behavior while also thinking that he is being unnecessarily provoked. Or, you may be angry with the school for not making enough special allowances for your child.

Your heart bleeds for him as you watch him struggle. But you may also be tempted to be too strict with him because his behavior makes you look bad. Or you may be tempted to be too lenient to compensate for how hard life is for him during school hours, or just to get a break from the constant conflict with him.

Unfortunately, your embarrassment, anger at the school, and heartache over his struggles are probably not your only responses. You are also probably frustrated with him because, being a typical teenager, he brings home his anger over what happens at school. Maybe he has blamed you, as his parent, for his problems. He may also refuse your help. Or he may even deny that he has a challenge at all!

Your child may also have less ability to cope with the normal emotions of adolescence, and yet struggles with the same desires for independence as kids without these challenges. Because of his situation, he may be far more influenced by peer pressure than other kids and thus make more bad choices. He may also be upset with you if you try to convince him that his "friends" are using him or are amusing themselves at his expense.

Your child may have gone so far as to turn to drug abuse for peer acceptance, or to blunt the pain of school and social failure. Perhaps he did not start out with any special impediments, but rebellious behavior and drug abuse have helped *produce* troubles such as mood or anxiety problems.

If your child has been placed on medicine, you probably have additional questions about how to deal with him. Does his being on medicine mean that he has a disease and cannot help behaving the way he does? Should a child on medicine be held to a different standard of attitude and behavior than a child who isn't? In answering these questions, we'll find it helpful to see what the Bible teaches about our child's physical and spiritual makeup.

Both Body and Heart

The Bible teaches that we are duplex beings—that is, we are made up of a body or outer person, and a spirit or inner person.

This inner person, which the Bible often refers to as the "heart," is the part of us that thinks, feels, and chooses.

Because we are not bodiless spirits, our bodies mediate (respond to or express) our thoughts, feelings, and choices. This results in our physical responses, speech, and behavior. Jesus taught this when he said, "The good man out of the good treasure of his heart brings forth what is good; and the evil man out of the evil treasure brings forth what is evil; for his mouth speaks from that which fills his heart" (Luke 6:45 NASB). Our bodies, in turn, can also profoundly influence our thoughts, feelings, and choices.

In contrast to biblical teaching, the prevailing view among many scientists and doctors is that we consist of only one part, our body. This view is based upon a philosophy called "materialism," the belief that the material world (that which we can sense and measure scientifically) is all that there is. A consistent materialist does not believe in God, the afterlife, or the inner man.

Although Christians do not believe that the material world is all there is, we often behave as if we are materialists in the area of health. We believe in God and the inner man, but when we go to a doctor we may not think critically about what he tells us. Instead, we may take a view about our body's health that leaves out the spiritual dimension.

A materialist believes that the brain is the organ in our body that thinks, feels, and makes choices. He believes that how it thinks and what it chooses depends solely upon the balance or imbalance of its chemicals. A materialist would say that what we experience as consciousness is simply a manifestation of the activity of the brain.

This belief is based upon a large amount of research that shows a connection between our brain's function and our thoughts, emotions, and behavior. This scientific data is true and valid. But the materialistic view is a *belief, an interpretation of the data* based upon assumptions that there *is* no *God* or invisible reality, and that this world is all there is. Although it is based upon facts, this belief is not itself a fact—it is a belief. It is also contrary to the teaching of the Word of God about the nature of man.

In the Christian worldview, all scientific data must be interpreted beginning with the assumption that the Bible is true. By looking at the same data through the lens of Scripture, we arrive at a very different conclusion. The Bible teaches that our heart, or invisible inner person, is the source of our thoughts and intentions (Hebrews 4:12), our emotions (Romans 9:2), and our choices (Matthew 15:18).

Our choices are expressed through the activity of our bodies, as when our mouth speaks from what fills our heart (Luke 6:45 and Matthew 12:24 NASB). The chemical balance and activity of our brain, which is the part of our body that initiates the speech that our mouth vocalizes, is therefore a *reflection* of what is going on in our heart, rather than the *source* of our thoughts, feelings, and behavior. The inner man, or heart, is the *source* of the outer, physical man's words and actions.

Dr. Edward Welch, a professor of practical theology and a biblical counselor, describes it this way:

> At the level of the brain, this unity (of body and inner man) suggests that the heart or spirit will always be *represented* or *expressed* in the brain's chemical activity. When we choose good or evil, such decisions will be accompanied by changes in brain activity. When we think about how to disciple our children, there will be unique brain activity. This does not mean that the brain *causes* these decisions. It simply means that the brain renders the desires of the heart in a physical medium. It is as if the heart always leaves its footprints on the brain.[2]

Does this mean that a sinful heart can produce actual disease in the body? Although Scripture does imply that there sometimes can be a connection between the state of our hearts and the health of our bodies (see, for example, 2 Samuel 13:2), a truth that science also affirms, it nowhere teaches a direct cause-and-effect relationship between the two. This is the lesson Job's "comforters" had to learn when they insisted that Job was sick because he had secret sin in his heart.

A materialist would say that a healthy brain generally produces happy feelings, comfortable thoughts, and good behavior. Bad feelings, thoughts, or behavior are viewed as disease, an uncomfortable and undesirable condition due to an unhealthy organ. Now, it is certainly true that the brain develops diseases like the rest of our body does. Alzheimer's disease, for example, causes physical changes in the cells of the brain, which lead to their death. But to define every bad feeling, uncomfortable thought, or bad behavior as a brain disease is very different and often incorrect.

If we were to apply this standard to our abdomen, for example, we would expect pain pills to cure the disease of appendicitis, rather than the removal of the inflamed appendix. Abdominal pain is a sign that something is wrong in our abdomen. It is not a disease in its own right. In the same way, emotional pain or distressing thoughts may be signs that something is not right with our hearts. In the same way that pain medicines will not cure appendicitis but will only cover up the signs, medicine directed at our emotions may only cover up the signs that we have "heart trouble."

Please understand that I am not arguing that there are no brain diseases that can lead to disordered behavior, or that to use medicines for these problems is always wrong. I will explore these matters in greater detail in chapter 7.

The materialistic view of the brain has other implications we need to be aware of. This view teaches that our feelings and behavior are determined by the activity of our brains alone. The logical conclusion, then, is that when we do wrong or feel bad, it must not be our fault. A disease must be responsible, not us. But this is not what the Bible teaches.

We are instructed repeatedly in Scripture to *choose* to do right. Our inner person is not at the mercy of our brain's chemical functions. We are told that when we choose to do right for the right reasons and motives, we feel better (Genesis 4:5-7). The Bible's instructions are meaningless if we are not able to choose our own behaviors, but rather, our actions are merely the result of a brain "disease."

A Balanced View of Our Child's Challenge

We can reason from the Bible's teachings about our child's body and heart to arrive at a balanced response to his dilemma. On the one hand, the Bible tells us that our child's bad behavior results from sin that starts in his heart. So when our child behaves badly, he has made a sinful choice and acted upon it. He may have made his sinful choice consciously and with full intent to do wrong, or without thinking his choice through, on the basis of habit. Either way, the Bible teaches that he is responsible for his choice and is guilty of sin.

On the other hand, it is possible for bodily weakness to have an effect upon the activity of our child's inner person. For example, in 1 Kings 19 we see the effect that fear and physical exhaustion had on the prophet Elijah. Having successfully challenged the many false prophets of Baal, he had to flee for his life from Jezebel. Exhausted from his journey, Elijah wanted to give up. "I have had enough, LORD,' he said. 'Take my life'" (1 Kings 19:4 NIV). God ensured that he got food and rest, and later encouraged Elijah that all was not lost, and commissioned a helper for him.

Similarly, we have all observed that our children behave better and are less prone to discouragement when they have eaten properly and have had a good night's sleep. Although a hungry or sleepy body cannot *make* our child sin, it can make our child more vulnerable in his struggle against sin.

A child who is predisposed by his physical makeup to be inattentive does not have a disease in the sense that medical materialism defines it. He doesn't have a dysfunction of his brain that is the *cause* of his behavior. However, he may indeed have a physical weakness that will affect his ability to resist the sin of impulsive speech or action. Even so, he is still responsible to obey his teacher, be quiet, and stay in his seat, although he may find this much harder to do so than another student would.

There are also children whose bodies are seriously ill or injured, like those with diabetes or brain damage. No one would argue that these challenges are not diseases. Does this mean that these children's diseases are responsible for their sin? The Bible says no in their case, too. The physical body itself is still not the source of sinful attitudes and behavior; rather, the heart is. These children have sick bodies, but the problem with their choices is due to the fact that they have sinful hearts, just like the rest of us.

A child with diabetes sins, as does a child with brain damage. Children with both of these diseases may have special difficulties with resisting sin in the area of their physical weakness. The diabetic child may struggle with disobedience when he is hungry, much more seriously than a child without diabetes would struggle under the same circumstances. He needs to receive his meals and his insulin on schedule. The child with a brain injury may find it far more difficult to control certain kinds of impulses. He will need to receive a great deal of specialized help, both educational and medical.

A Right Response to Our Challenged Child

How do the Bible's teachings answer our questions about how much to expect from our challenged child? They tell us that we need to hold our challenged child responsible for his sin, *and* that genuine physical weakness may be a factor in his struggle against the temptation to make bad choices. We need to balance these two truths, placing the appropriate emphasis on each of them in any given situation. This requires careful discernment on our part.

It is important to remember that our child faces special pressures, such as the effect of learning difficulties and rejection by his classmates. He may also have less understanding of his situation and less ability to respond creatively to his problems. These factors don't excuse him when he makes bad choices, but as we consider their influence, we will remember to be especially gentle and understanding when we find that we must correct him.

We as parents can be tempted to make bad choices of our own in response to our child's choices. We may be tempted to excuse or minimize a child's bad behavior, failing to hold him responsible for sinful choices because of the special burden he carries. Or, exasperated and embarrassed by his behavior, we may take a hard-line approach, insisting that he meet our standards without trying to understand his genuine weakness.

Both of these "one size fits all" approaches will fail to meet God's standard. When we excuse or minimize bad behavior, we are failing to insist upon obedience to God's commands. But when we take a hard-line approach, we are failing to temper our justice with mercy.

The Bible gives us guidance that enables us to navigate the territory between these two extremes; let's explore what it has to say about parenting challenged kids.

No Exception for Challenged Children

People with various challenges are found throughout Scripture, so their presence among God's people is presumed, but we are given no special instructions other than the command not to take advantage of them (for example, see Deuteronomy 27:18). The conclusion that we should draw, based upon what is absent from the Scriptures as well as what is present, is that God intends that there should be one standard of behavior for all people, rather than a separate standard for people who may have certain physical or mental obstacles to overcome.

Does it make sense to you that there is no exception for our challenged children in Scripture? Consider these truths about them: They are descendants of Adam, created in the image of God, just like the rest of us (Genesis 1:26-27). Because of Adam's sin, they too are born with a sinful nature (Psalm 51:5), just as we are, and sin (Romans 3:23) just as we do. We are commanded to raise them in the discipline and instruction of the Lord (Ephesians 6:4). They need a Savior (Romans 5:6-10), just as we do. The characteristics that our challenged children have in common with us are far more important than the characteristics that are different.

But It's Harder for My Child to Obey!

One of the characteristics that our challenged child has in common with us is the temptation he faces. The Bible tells us that our child's temptations are "common to man" (1 Corinthians 10:13). This means that he faces the same temptations as everyone else. This is a truth that we may need to work hard to accept. The ways our child is tempted may seem very different from the ways we are tempted, but God's Word tells us that there are no unique temptations.

Though it may seem to us that it is so much harder for our child to obey God than it is for us to do so, Scripture says that his situation is not so different from ours. Rather, in the same way that we must learn how to resist temptation so that we can honor and glorify God, our child must learn to do battle when he is tempted to make bad choices.

God's Word also tells us that when our problem is greater, the grace that God gives to deal with the problem will also be greater. For example, when the apostle Paul experienced a weakness that he referred to as a "thorn in the flesh," he prayed to God three times, asking Him to take it away. Paul reports that God told him, "My grace is sufficient for you, for my power is made perfect in weakness" (2 Corinthians 12:9). God did not take away the weakness, but promised Paul the extra grace he needed. In the same book, Paul tells us, "And God is able to make all grace abound to you, so that in all things at all times, having all that you need, you will abound in every good work" (2 Corinthians 9:8 NIV).

Some of our children will find it hard to think about what God commands before they act. Some will struggle with overwhelming desires to do things that are not good. Some will have difficulty remembering or understanding what God requires. Some will find it easy to become sinfully despondent or lose hope. As we guide them to remember God's standard for their behavior, we must do so with gentleness and encouragement, always turning them to Christ, reminding them that God understands their struggles and that He gives the power to obey to those who ask Him for it.

Where Does Sin End and Weakness Begin?

As we work to hold our child accountable for his wrong choices, we may find it difficult to distinguish intentional sin from a wrong choice that was influenced by our child's special area of weakness, or was even a mistake. At the same time that we need to be careful not to excuse sin, we must remember that not every wrong choice is intentionally sinful.

Even if our child is rebellious, he may, in a given instance, have made a mistake. Kids with developmental and cognitive-perceptual challenges[3] are especially prone to misinterpreting and misunderstanding because of the nature of their problems. Our child may also have been acting habitually without thinking his choice through. Although he is still responsible for his wrong choice, his weaknesses should be considered when deciding what discipline is appropriate for a given circumstance.

One common problem is when an inattentive child fails to listen as instructions are given, and thus does not realize what is required of him. Here he was responsible to do something that he did not do, yet was capable of doing. He failed to pay the necessary attention to learn what was required of him, and this is why he failed to obey. But a genuine weakness on his part made it more difficult for him to choose to pay attention to instructions.

How sinful was the choice he made? Only God, who understands our child's heart, knows whether he made a conscious choice not to pay attention or simply "spaced out" and honestly didn't hear what he was told to do. Or, he may have a sinful habit of failing to listen. He may have even deliberately chosen to disobey and plead his weakness as an excuse.

Challenged kids can learn to get out of unpleasant tasks by claiming they don't understand or "can't" do what is required of them. They can fail to give sufficient attention or effort to the job they have been asked to do. They can learn to do an incomplete or sloppy job, using their challenge as an excuse for their failure and expecting others to finish or fix their work. If our child adopts habitual behavior patterns like these and they are not addressed, he will have difficulty in adult life.

It is important to correct our child's behavior when we see patterns like these, and we should not be content to stop with mere correction. Our goal should be to understand the *why* as well as the *what* of his behavior. If we have a habit of gentle, patient communication with our child, he is more likely to be honest as we seek to understand him. We don't just want to know why he does the things he does; we also want to help *him* understand himself better. This is the first step in helping a child to turn from any sinful heart motivations that may be driving his behavior.[4]

If our communications have not been characterized by gentleness and patience in the past, asking his forgiveness for our own sinful heart attitudes can help reopen the communication lines. It's never too late to start communicating with him in a new way.

We will want to remember that love thinks the best of others (1 Corinthians 13:7) as we seek to understand the reasons for our child's behavior. In cases where we are not able to determine this for whatever reason, we still can motivate him to do his best job by establishing predictable consequences for failing to obey.

Structured Discipline Will Encourage Obedience

The Bible teaches us that our choices have predictable consequences. We are told repeatedly that when we make good choices, God's blessings will rest on us. This principle is clearly stated in chapters 28 through 30 of Deuteronomy, where God tells us that the positive outcome of obedience is blessing, and the negative consequence of disobedience is a curse.

Although none of us always chooses to do good, we can still teach our children the blessings of trusting in the righteousness of Christ and resting in the finished work of Calvary. Jesus Christ, who alone always did what was right and who alone deserved God's blessing, took the curse that was due to us. We, and our children, can now pursue an obedience that flows from a heart of gratitude and we can embrace structure and discipline (when we fail) as part of God's means of helping us grow. We must teach the biblical principle of gracious obedience to our child, and reinforce it by consistently holding him to a standard that is appropriate to his level of challenge, all the while encouraging him to trust in the perfect obedience of the Son.

I (Laura) struggled with finding the right balance in these very matters as our son grew up. He was very inattentive when he was small. I found it difficult to discipline him because my sympathy for his weakness tempted me to make exceptions for him. But I learned that insisting upon a minimum standard with a predictable consequence was kinder to him in the long run because it motivated him to improve in his areas of weakness. I found that he would apply himself to mastering difficult tasks when it was not easy for him to get out of doing them. His attention capacities improved as he gave a full effort, and as his attention improved, I was able to slowly increase my expectations of him.

His condition improved markedly over the years, one small step at a time. When he was diagnosed with autism at age three, we were told that he was retarded. At the time of this writing, he had finished tenth grade in a Christian school with a straight-A average. I can't promise that every challenged child will experience this degree of success, but if consistent and balanced training in the area of attention can improve an autistic child this much, it can help many kids with less severe challenges.

Ultimately, those of us who have kids with special challenges have the same goal as all other parents. We want to set a gentle but uncompromising standard of obedience to God's commands before our children, understanding their special areas of weakness, and always pointing them to the cross for the power to live the way that God commands.

Psalm 103:13-14 says that "as a father shows compassion to his children, so the LORD shows compassion to those who fear him. For he knows our frame; he remembers that we are dust." God's standard for our behavior is always high, but because He understands our weaknesses, He gently and patiently enables us to achieve His standard by His grace. Let's seek to model our parenting after our Father's example.

Born to Glorify God

In John chapter 9, the Lord Jesus Christ was asked a question about an adult who had a severe physical problem. His disciples wanted to know whether a man who was born blind was being punished for his own or for his parents' sin. How painful that question must have been for the man and his parents! Not only were they living with a handicap, but the disciples suggested that *someone* must be to blame for it.

Those of us who have challenged kids often receive comments about our child that reflect the same kind of attitude. Some people judge us for our child's failures. They assume that we or something we've done is to blame for our child's condition.

In the face of such censure, we can find encouragement in Jesus' explanation for the blind's man's condition. He said that the man was born blind "so that the works of God might be displayed in him" (John 9:3). Far from assigning blame to the man or his parents, Jesus' focus was where ours needs to be—on what *God* is doing.

We can be comforted by the sure knowledge that God sees and understands our hard work, sacrifice, and struggle with a difficult child. And our children can be comforted with the knowledge that God knows infallibly the difference between their limitations and their sin, even if we don't always. God is full of mercy for the weak and suffering.

Notice that the blind man in John 9—who appeared to most people to be under God's curse—became the recipient of a great honor: the opportunity to be healed by the Messiah and to come to faith in Him as a result. He heard Jesus say, "As long as I am in the world, I am the light of the world" (John 9:5). After he was healed, the man glorified God further by the testimony of his faith in Christ before the Jewish leaders in Jerusalem.

All of us who love a challenged child can find comfort in the knowledge that our children, like the man born blind, were designed by their Creator to glorify Him. Most of our challenged children will glorify God through the patient endurance of their challenge. Some may glorify Him by defying the limited expectations their doctors and parents had for them. All can glorify God by the faith that they learn in the crucible of adversity. All have the opportunity to testify to the lordship of Jesus Christ in their lives in the same way as the man who was born blind.

Does this seem impossible to you now as your child takes his frustration over his challenges out on you and resists your authority? Do you wonder if your child will ever learn to respond to his challenges in a way that glorifies God? Do you fear that your challenged child will never make the change from rebellion to mature faith?

God does not call us to be successful parents. He calls us to be faithful parents. As we trust in His providence and pray for wisdom to address our child's challenges faithfully, considering his weaknesses, we, too, will glorify God by our obedience. We also will provide the environment in which our child will be most likely to learn to glorify God in his own struggles with his challenges.

Please take time to ask the Lord to help you see how your child was created to glorify Him, and then ask Him to give you wisdom as you work through the questions that follow.

Growing in Hope, Discovering His Help

1. Are you overly harsh or rigid in your parenting approach to your challenged child? Does your embarrassment over his behavior make it harder to understand and sympathize with his weakness? In what areas do you need to go to God in prayer for patience and flexibility?

2. Do you think like a materialist about your child's challenge? Have you concluded that he "can't help" his choices? How can a biblical view of his makeup help to balance your response to his behavior?

3. Have you been treating your child as "exempt" from God's standard? In what areas do you need to adhere to God's standards and/or implement predictable consequences for failures?

4. In four or five sentences, summarize what you've learned in this chapter.

7

Will Medicine Help
My Child?

Dr. Laura Hendrickson

If any of you lacks wisdom, let him ask God, who
gives generously to all without reproach,
and it will be given him.
—JAMES 1:5

———

I (Laura) heard a very telling comment the other day. A doctor said, "Someone tell me how to get through the year coaching Little League baseball without putting myself on Xanax,[1] half the kids on antidepressants, the other half on Ritalin,[2] and some of the parents on antipsychotic medication."[3] Although this statement was made in jest and I laughed, still, it reflects what has become a growing problem in our society. That is, we tend to rely on medicine to help control or cure our feelings rather than learn how to cope with them.

Psychiatric medicines can be useful tools. But as we learned in chapter 6, bad thoughts and feelings are not, in and of themselves, diseases. Medicine is not the only, or even the best, way to help a child cope with bad thoughts and feelings. Just because a medicine makes a challenged child act or feel better does not mean that he has a disease, or that he *needs* the medicine to help change his feelings or behavior.

Please do not misunderstand me. There *are* true brain diseases. I would never advocate withholding medicine from a suffering child, especially if there were no other ways to ease his suffering. But when we suggest that the answer to all of our children's difficult behaviors and feelings is in a pill, we may actually end up harming them. Again, please don't misunderstand. I am not saying that giving psychiatric medicines to challenged children is always a wrong choice. But seeing medicine *alone* as the answer to our children's challenges is wrong, because our children are more than just bodies. They are also invisible, living souls.

What Can We Expect from a Medicine?

A medicine can change a child's feelings. It can also improve his concentration and self-control. It can suppress hallucinations, things he might see or hear that aren't really there. It can decrease anxiety. These are real changes that can occur in his brain when he takes psychiatric medicines.

But a medicine cannot teach a child to choose to think thoughts leading to peace and happiness instead of thoughts leading to anxiety or depression. Medicine cannot train his brain to pay attention, or learn self-control. A medicine can only suppress bad thoughts, feelings, and behavior. It cannot teach a child to choose differently in his heart, choices that the Bible teaches will lead to different thoughts, feelings, and behavior.

While medicine may be needed for the control of a few severe brain conditions, better behavior, self-control, and emotional stability can be learned by almost all children. Before we choose medications for our child, we need to be sure we are making the best choice for his long-term welfare.

Medicate or Train the Brain?

A child's brain develops in response to the ways it is habitually used, and as it develops, we see physical and mental skills emerge. This is why sports-minded fathers like to introduce their little boys to tiny soccer balls and batting tees long before they are big enough for youth sports. This is also why we work with our children carefully from an early age to teach them how to read.

But our society is far more concerned with physical and intellectual ability than it is with behavioral and emotional competence. We don't tend to think of the ability to concentrate or cope with uncomfortable feelings as skills. Most of us wouldn't have any idea of how to teach these skills even if we did think of them in that way. When our children reach school age and begin to have difficulty paying attention or develop upsetting habits of behavior or thought, our first reaction is usually to send them to the doctor, who frequently prescribes a medicine. Is there another way?

There is a large amount of scientific data suggesting that children with many kinds of behavioral and emotional problems can improve in the areas of their weaknesses through focused training. Techniques that teach depressed and anxious people to change the beliefs they hold about themselves and their problems[4] have good success rates. There are also techniques for dealing with obsessive thoughts (thoughts you can't get out of your head), and compulsive behaviors (things you feel you can't help doing).[5] A number of nonmedical alternatives for training attentiveness and improving learning also exist.[6]

These secular methods are generally consistent with what God's Word teaches about our thoughts, feelings, and behaviors, and how we change. As we learned in chapter 6, the Bible teaches that what we think and the choices we make produce changes in our feelings and our behavior. In addition, the Bible promises us that just committing our family to a lifestyle of obedience to God's Word will help with a variety of different challenges.

How Can I Help My Child with His Specific Challenge?

I find it helpful to group the various kinds of challenges a child can face into basic types, each of which has its own kinds of problems and possible solutions. As we understand the common elements in each group, it is easier to see what kinds of solutions may help each unique child. This chapter describes five basic types of challenge and discusses ways to help a child with each one.

Academic and Behavioral Challenges

These are probably the most common challenges. Your child may have difficulty sitting still or paying attention in class, and may be sloppy and inattentive at home. His level of academic achievement may be below that of his peers, even though he is trying very hard to do well. Some kids find it much more difficult than others to pay attention, to be well organized, and to keep their room clean. Others are very physical and active by nature. It can be torture to sit still in school all day if this is not your natural inclination. Kids with this complication can also be impatient, impulsive, and short-tempered.

You may have been told that your child suffers from a brain chemical imbalance disease, and that he requires Ritalin to function normally. You may be vaguely uneasy about this, on the one hand wanting to give your child every possible opportunity, but on the other feeling that many of his problems are of his own making. Or, you may have made the medicine decision long ago and found that although your child's schoolwork has improved, his behavior still leaves a lot to be desired. Is there anything more that can be done?

The two areas that need to be addressed in these kinds of children are attention and behavior. Attention can be improved with various kinds of focused training. Because impulsivity, impatience, and other sins of the heart produce sinful behaviors, these heart issues also need to be addressed. Many of the principles presented in this book will help improve behavior in the home, and a good choice of school will provide the consistency needed for the rest of your child's day.

A Christian school with a traditional curriculum may be more helpful for your child than a public school with special education tracking. The Christian school usually provides discipline, consistency, and consequences based upon a biblical worldview. Traditional instruction methods that involve phonics, memory work, and skills drills in math can help many children who have learning difficulties. Although you may have heard that traditional methods are not helpful for children with these problems, I have seen many challenged learners, including my own son, do well with these methods.

Homeschooling should not be ruled out either, even if there is rebellion in your home. For kids with serious learning difficulties or poor attention skills, it could be the best choice. Some children have been so hurt by their academic difficulties and negative peer experiences that coming home to work at their own pace can be a great relief. Others need more consistency and discipline geared to their needs than can be provided in a public school. And if you can't afford a private school, then consider schooling at home.

Regular physical exercise has been shown to improve attention. Organized team sports provide structured activity and an opportunity for inattentive kids to burn off energy. Dance, gymnastics, and karate classes can help build the coordination and attention skills of less physically talented or "drifty" kids. Children with serious physical clumsiness, learning difficulties, and attention problems can benefit from structured physical activities directed by an occupational therapist.[7]

Although you may not have thought of physical activity as providing training for your inattentive child, every time your child is engaged in a structured activity, he is practicing paying attention and building new connections in his brain. He also has less time for the electronic activities that have been linked to poor attention.[8] Children with less exposure to television, computers, and video games are more attentive and are better readers.

Some parents have found that focused tutoring helps their challenged child keep up in school. Others have found that eye exercises known as visual training, offered by some eye doctors, improve attention and school performance.

Attention training using biofeedback is also available. Biofeedback works by measuring brain waves. An inattentive child's brain waves are measured, and he is taught techniques to help him pay better attention. As he watches the screen, the brain wave recordings tell him and his trainer if he is paying full attention. As he learns what paying full attention feels like, he is more able to achieve this state by concentrating.

All of these options for improving attention through physical training take time, money, and commitment, but have been effective with some kids. If your child is already taking medicines, perhaps he could be successfully weaned off of them with the help of some of these attention-building activities.

The most important question you should ask a doctor who wants to prescribe a medicine to improve your child's attention is, "How long do you anticipate my child being on this medicine?" If he tells you that your child has a lifelong disorder that will always require medical treatment, I suggest that you get another opinion. You want to find a doctor who sees medicines, if used at all, as one temporary part of an overall training plan designed to help improve your child's ability to pay attention rather than as a permanent solution to a supposed disease that cannot be cured. A doctor who is committed to getting to the source of your child's problem should be able to suggest supplemental or alternative treatments like the ones I've mentioned in this section.

Medicines that are used to treat inattention have been associated with the development of problems far more serious than poor attention. Please refer to Appendix C to find out more about the serious side-effects of these medicines.

I also recommend that you receive biblical counsel from your pastor or a biblical counselor.[9] As parents receive biblical counsel for themselves and their children, they learn to order their lives to give more consistency and stability to their children.

Anxiety and Habit Challenges

These nervous children have habits that may have made them feel better at first, but over time, the habits have become serious problems. Your child may pick at his face, pull out his hair, or twitch when he is worried. She may diet excessively or vomit up food to keep from gaining weight. He may be obsessed with unusual worries and feel the need to repeat certain actions over and over to feel safe. All of these behaviors are in response to anxious feelings, and they can lead to enslavement to certain habits of thought and action.

These habits can easily take up more and more of your child's time, making it harder for him to do homework, do chores, or play. In time, the habits will no longer make him feel better, but instead, produce more anxiety. This new anxiety sometimes leads to the appearance of additional habits. If a child has bald spots on his head or goes to the bathroom five times an hour to wash his hands, he may be teased by other kids, which, in turn, adds to the burden that he bears.

If your child has been prescribed medicine for a problem and the problem has gone away, he is one of a very small minority. Typically medicines give some relief for a time, but they are not a true or complete solution. Often the symptoms will return or worsen, making it necessary to increase the dosage or add a second medicine. Is this the best that can be done for your child? Will he live for the rest of his life like this?

The Bible teaches us that the thoughts a person thinks on the inside lead to the actions he takes and the words he speaks (Matthew 12:33-35). So to help your child break the habit of anxious actions, you need to help him break the habit of thinking anxious thoughts.

Kids who express their anxiety through behavior such as hair pulling,[10] muscle twitching,[11] or self-injury can greatly improve when they are encouraged to talk about their worries and receive specific help designed to break their habit. They also need to learn to correct their habits of thought about themselves, their needs, their desires, and other people's opinions of them based upon what God's Word says about these subjects.

For example, those who express anxiety over their appearance through obsessive dieting or vomiting need help understanding how their concern is focused on the wrong thing. Jesus said that if our primary focus is on pleasing God, He takes care of the other, less important things that we worry about (Matthew 6:25-34).

All anxious kids can benefit from understanding that God's solution for their problem is, "Don't worry; pray about it, instead."[12] God's Word goes on to tell us in Philippians 4:7 that when we do this thankfully, "the peace of God, which surpasses all understanding, will guard your hearts and your minds in Christ Jesus."

Some kids have thoughts "stuck" in their heads that may seem crazy or repulsive to them, but that they cannot get rid of (obsessions). These kids may feel that they need to take certain actions to get rid of the thoughts (compulsions). But the more they act on the thoughts, the more they think them and feel the need to act on them.

Recent research suggests that when a person caught in this trap chooses to refuse the thought and its action instead of giving in to it, he can begin to break this habit of thought. A book[13] about this research shows pictures of an area of disordered function in the brain, seen on a special brain scan, which normalizes when sufferers refuse to think obsessive thoughts.

As a former psychiatrist who is now a biblical counselor, I am excited about this physical evidence, which agrees with scriptural teachings on the connection between our thoughts, feelings, and behavior. This evidence affirms the value of the biblical counseling approach, as taught in Scripture. It also agrees with recent advances in the field of brain research known as neuroplasticity,[14] which have shown that when we choose to think differently, our brain begins to change its function and even its connections.[15]

When a doctor wants to give your child medicine for an anxiety problem, ask, "How will taking this medicine teach him not to think the anxious thoughts that lead to his anxious habits?" A doctor who does not see a link between what your child is thinking and how he is behaving will not be able to help your child change his thoughts. I strongly recommend counseling by a qualified biblical counselor for kids with this problem.

Some doctors recommend antidepressant medicine as a temporary help for a person who is learning to cope with an anxiety problem during the early stages of making that change. Before you decide that this is what you want to do for your child, be sure you have carefully considered the information I have compiled on these drugs in Appendix C. These medicines have the potential to bring about serious and dangerous side effects.

Emotional Challenges

Children with emotional challenges often suffer from sadness or unstable moods. They may be happy one day and blue the next, or unhappy for weeks or months at a time. Often, the sadness and mood swings are in response to rejection from peers, or a difficult situation at home. Kids with serious illnesses are also more prone to depression due to physical weakness.

Sometimes illegal drugs, alcohol, or even prescribed medicines can produce these sorts of mood changes. Mania, a sleepless and extremely hyperactive condition, can result from sleep loss, substance abuse, or even psychiatric medicine. The diagnosis of bipolar disorder has recently become a popular psychiatric label for children who have strong mood swings.

Children with these challenges frequently face peer difficulties at school. Their problem coping with their emotions may make them the focal point of jokes at school. As these kids struggle with their emotions their schoolwork can suffer, and this gives them yet another reason to become depressed or anxious.

The preteen and teen years are a time of strong emotions. We parents understand this, and tend to attribute these emotions to the hormonal changes that come with maturing. Yet we must keep in mind that nobody is a passive victim of their own hormones— even though parents may sometimes feel like victims of their children's hormones!

The Bible tells us that the fruit of the Spirit is self-control (Galatians 5:22). This means that a believer, even a child or teen, will develop self-control and other virtues as he abides in Christ. But self-control develops in us just like any other skill—through practice. Most teenagers, even those who are very serious about their faith, struggle with self-control.

A teen experimenting with rebellious behaviors or struggling with a difficult living circumstance may have a hard time with his emotions. If he does not yet have saving faith in Christ, he has not yet entered the relationship that makes self-control and other Christian virtues possible.

We parents can do a lot to help our emotionally troubled children cope by providing a consistent and understanding home environment. But if our child is experiencing emotional instability because we are emotionally unstable ourselves, or because our home environment is chaotic, we need to get help for our own problems at the same time that we get help for our child.

Sometimes family members in a troubled home assume that if a "problem" child gets help, the rest of the family's problems will be solved. But just because a child manifests behavioral or emotional instability does not mean that the child is the only one with a problem, or that solving that child's problem will produce peace in the home. A child's problems may actually bring to light some of our own —and his improvement may depend upon our ability to bring our *own* behavior under control.

Because emotions of depression or excitement are, like anxious feelings, a product of the thoughts our child chooses to think, the emotionally unstable child needs to be taught to correct his thoughts in accord with the teachings in God's Word. Biblical counseling will be very helpful for the child with an emotional challenge. Often the whole family can benefit from this.

Some kids with emotional challenges are tempted to abuse alcohol or street drugs to blunt the emotional pain they feel, and kids who are abusing alcohol or street drugs often have mood swings. We must be sure that our emotionally challenged child has not fallen into this trap. His emotional weakness will not improve if he is abusing drugs and alcohol.

If your doctor wants to prescribe an antidepressant for your child, the main question to ask is, "How will this medicine help my child learn to cope better with his feelings?" If your doctor thinks that your child may be at risk for suicide, or if your child is not responding well to counseling, a limited time on an antidepressant could be considered. But the Food and Drug Administration (FDA) has recently publicized the potential danger of increased suicidal thinking in children and teenagers taking antidepressants.[16] Parents should weigh the risks and benefits carefully.

Whenever medicines can be avoided, they should be. A child is not learning to cope when a pill temporarily takes the painful emotions away, and these drugs may be dangerous. Please turn to Appendix C for information on medicines prescribed for emotional instability.

If your doctor wants to prescribe a mood-stabilizing drug for your child, you will want to ask him the same question as for antidepressants: "How will this medicine help my child learn how to cope better with his feelings?" If your child has mood swings that alternate between unhappiness and mild excitement, he has unstable *emotions*, not a disease.

Although mood-stabilizing drugs do not have the same serious side effects as antidepressants, children generally are prescribed both of these medicines together. Because mood-stabilizing drugs, like antidepressants, change the feelings but do not address the root cause of the problem, counseling is a much better approach for children who are emotionally challenged.

On the other hand, I have seen people whose alcohol or drug abuse produced an episode of mania. Antidepressant treatment is also known to produce mania as a side effect. Sleeplessness because of "cram sessions" before tests can also precipitate this problem, which can induce a true medical emergency. If your child has become sleepless and excited to the extent that he is displaying seriously psychotic (that is, "crazy") thoughts, a stay in a psychiatric hospital and medicines may be needed in order to protect his life or the lives of others.

If your child has had an episode of this kind of mania, he may be kept on mood stabilizers for a period of time after the episode is over, and later, the medication dosage can be reduced slowly. You will want to work with your child to help him develop a more structured life while he is still on the medicine. He needs to learn to plan ahead for tests and get eight hours of sleep every night. He must give up all illegal drugs, and should also abstain from alcohol. I also recommend that he receive biblical counseling to help him develop better self-control.

A trial of medicine withdrawal should always be considered once your child's emotions have stabilized, because not all "crazy" behavior is brain disease. Some behavior like this is temporary, especially if prompted by substance abuse or sleep deprivation. I have seen people with a history of mania do well after being weaned off medicines when they have been taught mature coping skills and how to make choices that lead to greater stability.

Some people develop repeated periods of mania after a single episode. Because of the tremendous devastation that recurrences can produce, people who have had one recurrence may choose to take mood stabilizers for an extended time to prevent recurrences.

Cognitive-Perceptual Challenges

Your child may have a physical disease that is causing his brain to deteriorate, something similar to Alzheimer's disease. Or perhaps your child has been diagnosed with schizophrenia, a brain disease of unknown cause characterized by psychotic ("crazy") thoughts, hearing voices, and seeing things.

Cognitive-perceptual challenges are true brain diseases. The "cognitive" part of this name refers to the loss of intelligence that is usually a part of this challenge. The "perceptual" part refers to disturbances in the ability to tell what is real. Many children with cognitive-perceptual challenges have hallucinations—they hear or see things that are not really there.

A few psychiatrists and counselors maintain that because we do not know the exact disease process that produces schizophrenia,[17] we cannot know for certain that schizophrenia is a brain disease. I am confident that it is a brain disease because we see hallucinations and deterioration of intelligence in other conditions that produce abnormal function in the brain, such as brain tumors, brain infections, and traumatic brain injury.[18] Conversely, the deterioration of intelligence never occurs without a physical reason.

The thoughts of a child with hallucinations do not make sense to anyone but him, and they can be genuinely tormenting. Are these crazy thoughts due to his sin? While the Bible says that our hearts are indeed sinful, when signs of brain disease like these are involved in our child's problems, we need to exercise great discernment and compassion, remembering that only God truly understands everything about the interaction between our physical bodies and our hearts.

Let's recall our biblical model, which tells us that our thoughts come from our inner person and result in behavior that is expressed through our bodies. Our bodies, in turn, influence the thoughts, feelings, and choices of our inner person. So our biblical model suggests that perhaps thoughts are crazy when a diseased brain presents a misinterpretation of reality to the inner person. Because the thoughts are crazy, the behavior that results from the thoughts is crazy, too.

Are you familiar with the movie *A Beautiful Mind*? In it we see the breakdown of a man with schizophrenia, from his point of view. He thinks he sees someone chasing him, when in reality all he sees is a shadow. His belief that he is being followed is based upon what his brain tells him is happening, so he runs and hides. This is a rather simplified illustration of the process by which a brain disease may produce the symptoms we observe, but it can help us to understand some of the behaviors and choices that characterize this type of problem.

This does not mean that we can rule out sin as a possible factor involved in the wrong choices of a child with a cognitive-perceptual challenge. Like the child with diabetes or brain injury that I referred to in chapter 6, a child with a disease in his brain has sin in his heart, just like the rest of us. But when the disease is cognitive-perceptual in nature, we must be especially patient when dealing with sinful tendencies, recognizing how little we understand about the connection between our child's disease and his sin.

Biblical counseling can help a child with this challenge, but he will not benefit fully from it unless his disease is brought under control so he can think clearly. In cases where a brain tumor can be removed or a brain infection can be treated with antibiotics, psychiatric medicines are not needed. But where the cause is not known and the disease cannot be cured, antipsychotic medicine generally helps to control the child's thoughts and behavior.

We must also remember that our child can complain of hallucinations without actually having them, either because he is being intentionally dishonest or because he is upset and not describing his experiences accurately. Because of this, I think that medicines should be scaled back slowly after a child's behavior has stabilized after a first episode of "crazy" behavior.

Occasionally a person will have an isolated episode of psychosis without mania that resolves itself and never returns, either because it was brought on by drug abuse or sleep deprivation, or for unknown reasons. But it is an unfortunate fact that some children will continue to have hallucinations and disturbed thoughts if they do not continue to receive medicines. Careful consultation with your doctor will enable you to weigh the risks and the benefits of continued treatment with antipsychotic medicines in your child's case. Please refer to Appendix C for more information on these drugs.

Traumatic Brain Injuries and Developmental Challenges

Traumatic brain injuries (TBI) are a type of brain damage caused by a severe blow to the head. Developmental challenges are serious problems that your child is born with, such as mental retardation and autism. Lower-functioning members of this group may be unable to speak or to dress without help, and often have seizures. Higher-functioning members may also learn on a retarded level. Some others may have a normal or even a high IQ while still having other serious difficulties.

Developmentally challenged teenagers and those with traumatic brain injury can be overwhelmed by anxiety and have difficulty responding appropriately when angry. They can become aggressive or even physically violent when teased. Self-control can be especially difficult for these kids.

Kids with these challenges respond well to structured cognitive training,[19] or in the case of TBI, retraining. My son received early intervention for his autism, with the result that today, he functions on the level of children without autism. This is an unusually good outcome, but the function of most developmentally challenged children will improve at least somewhat with this kind of training. Kids with TBI, like adults who have suffered a stroke, receive rehabilitation after their injury in an attempt to restore function that has been lost because of the injury.

This training is the reason that those suffering from these challenges generally live in their homes today rather than in an institution, as was common in earlier generations. Outcomes for kids with these kinds of challenges have markedly improved in recent years.

If your child has recently been diagnosed with one of these problems, you may have been offered medications to help you control his behavior. If so, you should ask your doctor if some form of cognitive training might be worth pursuing.

When our son was diagnosed with autism, we were offered medicines to produce improvements in core autistic symptoms, such as poor sleep and hyperactivity. As a psychiatrist who was aware of the side effects these medicines can produce, I was unwilling to begin using medicines unless it was clear that we had no other choice. In fact, our son never did receive psychiatric medicines because his attention, sleep, and behavior all improved once we began the early intervention training with him.

Many researchers in the field of neuroplasticity believe that this sort of training causes new connections to develop in an autistic child's brain—connections that improve the child's impairments. Whenever training can produce a change like this without medicine, it should be tried first. Medicines can be used to control a brain-injured or developmentally disabled child's behavior if training fails.

Some children with low function may become aggressive in adolescence, even if they were well-behaved when they were younger. It can be difficult for kids possessing a young mental age to understand the consequences of their choices and make the necessary effort to change, even with good biblical counsel and a consistent home environment. These children are sometimes placed on medicines that help control their behavior so they can remain home and in school. I recommend that before trying medicines, you seek biblical counsel for yourself as a parent as well as for your child. I have seen very difficult situations turn around when parents receive additional biblical help with a developmentally challenged child.

There are potentially serious side effects associated with the use of these medicines. A child who has limited ability to describe how a drug makes him feel can actually be made worse by a product intended to help him. For this reason, other options should be tried first before a decision is made to use such drugs.

Will Medicines Help My Child?

Generally speaking, medicine will help your child's symptoms, but he will not truly conquer his challenge without additional help. For this reason, an approach that emphasizes training rather than medicating, whenever possible, is a better choice. In some cases, medicine can be added as a temporary "jump start" to the counseling and training process, especially when your child is not coping well with his challenge. But in cases that involve severe disease or brain damage, medicines may need to be a permanent part of the help your challenged child receives.

If your child is already on medicines and you decide you would like to take him off of them, *you must do so under a doctor's supervision*. This is extremely important because stopping the medicines could lead to sudden distressing physical symptoms. Please see Appendix C for more information.

Our gracious heavenly Father, who is rich in wisdom and mercy, created your child for the same reason he created everyone else—to glorify Himself. It's our prayer that He will be glorified as you look to Him in prayer and trust Him with your precious child. May He also grant you wisdom as you seek to make the best choices in regard to helping your child.

Growing in Hope, Discovering His Help

1. What can we reasonably expect a medication to do? What should we not expect it to do?

2. How has this chapter changed the way that you think about psychiatric medication? What questions do you still have?

3. What are some of the training techniques mentioned in this chapter? What would be the benefit of using these techniques instead of a medicine?

4. In four or five sentences, summarize what you've learned in this chapter.

PART THREE

~

Dealing Wisely
with Your Children

8

The War for Their Souls

Fathers, do not provoke your children to anger,
but bring them up in the discipline and instruction of the Lord.
—EPHESIANS 6:4

What could be more precious than a soul? Could any possession or riches be of greater value to us than the souls of our beloved children? Jesus Himself taught that all the wealth in the entire world was nothing in comparison to the worth of just one soul (Mark 8:36)! Think about it. Could you measure the wealth of the entire world? Our children's souls have a worth beyond measure, and even though we may not think about this every day, we know it's true. As parents, we're in a battle for more than simple obedience to our rules. *We're in a spiritual war, a war for souls, and this war has eternal significance.*

Because you are reading this book, it's likely that you are suffering deeply over your child's spiritual captivity. Like you, we've lived through the nights of despair and sorrow. We've wept and doubted and racked our memories for signs of faith or glimmers of hope that our children's souls are safe. And we're all too acquainted with the bleak emptiness that fills our hearts when the days seem blackened by endless quarrels and the nights are cease-lessly clouded over with haunting fears. *What will happen to his soul? Will she suffer eternally? Oh God,* we pray, *be merciful.*

We know what it's like to suffer and to feel as though we've lost all hope; but we also know what it is to put our trust, our con-fidence, our hope in God. In chapter 1, we discovered that there are no foolproof methods or formulas we can follow that will absolutely guarantee our children's success. As we said, there are three factors that influence our children: we, his parents, his own heart, and the will of the sovereign Lord. Even then, even when all of our trust is in God alone, we can't excuse ourselves from our obligation to train and nurture our children. Even though only God is able to win this spiritual battle, He's asked us to fight with Him. This chapter (and this section of the book) will be about that fight and what your Commander has bid you to do. As we review His marching orders with you, remember that your only hope is in Him. Why not stop right now and ask Him to strengthen your heart and encourage your faith as we outline His battle plan? *Father,* you might pray, *help me to have faith to believe that You can change this situation, and give me the courage that I need to enter into the fray once again. Help me to love my child's soul more than I love peace, comfort, and rest. Equip my hands and fill my heart with courage. I pray these things for the sake of Your Son and in His name, Amen.*

No matter where you are in this process of defending your child's soul, God's directives are still applicable. Perhaps you've just endured your first wound and you're wondering how you should respond. Or maybe you're struggling to be faithful as the shattered remains of love, relationship, and home are piling up and you're wondering if it isn't just time to light the funeral pyre. Let us encourage you: *It's never too late for you to obey your heav-enly Commander.* It's never too late to apply principles from God's

Word—even if your children are nearing adulthood. Although the amount of influence you may have over your child does diminish as he grows, your faithful response to God's instruction must remain constant. Remember, although our hope is that our children will respond to God through our instruction, *we're only responsible for our obedience, not theirs.* While our children live, it's never too late to enter into the battle for their souls, no matter how many times we've crumbled in defeat or our enemy has won the skirmish.

Parenting Is a Lifelong Enlistment

The Bible is filled with the Lord's plan of war for souls. It focuses on the battle that His Son has already won for us on the cross and it also gives us directives about how to respond in the light of His victory. It tells us to understand, discipline, and train our children for the Lord and for the sake of their souls.

As we seek to develop a God-centered rather than a parent- or child-centered view of parenting, we can anticipate God's blessing as we humbly respond to His command to bear and raise children for Him (Genesis 1:28). One of the most well-known verses on child-rearing is found in Ephesians 6:4, where Paul writes, "Fathers, do not provoke your children to anger, but bring them up in the discipline and instruction of the Lord."

There are three principles evident in this verse that we'd like you to consider now (and in chapter 9) as you develop a God-centered battle plan for their souls. It's important that you...

- understand what your children really need from you so that they aren't provoked to anger;

- persist in your discipline as they grow (we'll look closely at discipline in chapter 9); and

- consistently train them for the Lord.

Fathers, This Is Your Job

Before we look at these three points, let's briefly consider the one to whom Paul addresses his admonitions. Paul speaks specifically to "fathers." In doing so, he isn't excusing mothers from his warning. But he *was* speaking to the head of the household—in much the same way that God gave commands to Adam, which were also binding upon Eve. Although it is true that God is speaking to both parents in Ephesians 6:4, and He is holding both parents accountable for their humble response, still, because fathers are the head or leader of the household, they carry the ultimate responsibility to guide and direct the family.

Although God has graciously offered to help us in the task of parenting, we have to come to grips with the fact that *parenting is our responsibility.* As fathers and mothers, it's easy to neglect our responsibilities and expect others, such as schools, peers, the media, or even the church to raise our kids and do the job God has called us to do. Raising our children is not a job that we can delegate to anyone else. God has assigned this mission to us, and as we seek to respond to Him in humble compliance, we can trust Him for His blessing on our work.

As we've said, parenting requires great sacrifice, and we parents know just how astounding and overwhelming those sacrifices can seem. From the time that little heart begins to beat within his mother's body, she's comprehending the sacrifices that will be expected of her. Her body is no longer her own. Her physical strength and her life will be absorbed by her baby as he grows within her and then demands his very sustenance from her. A father watches these changes and, with fear and trepidation, begins to understand the responsibilities that are soon to fall upon his shoulders. Before long he'll have another mouth to feed and he'll be called on to grow as a leader as his child looks to him for guidance, protection, and instruction. While the child matures and learns to understand his world, his parents are growing and learning, too—striving to keep up with his ever-increasing demands and their inability to predict what they will need to know next. Yes, parenting requires great sacrifices, and we wonder, *How can I be a good parent? How can I really understand my child and help him to grow in grace?*

Understanding What Your Child *Really* Needs

While it's important to seek to understand our kids and how they develop, much of the understanding that they really need is being overlooked. God, through the apostle Paul, warned fathers twice, "Fathers, do not provoke your children to anger" (Ephesians 6:4) and "Fathers, do not provoke your children, lest they become discouraged" (Colossians 3:21).

Understanding how our behavior and beliefs may cause our children to become habitually discouraged and angry is a significant part of following God into the battle for our children's souls.[1] We'll look briefly now at five of the most prevalent areas of misunderstanding that tempt our sons and daughters to become angry and rebellious. You might be surprised at some of these points, for they don't necessarily line up with what the popular culture will tell you that you need to know about parenting.

- lack of parental harmony
- failure to recognize the depth of our children's natural sinfulness
- parental neglect and overall busyness
- being emotionally distant and demanding
- overcontrol

Lack of Parental Harmony

One of the most disturbing influences upon children—one that will surely tempt them to sinful and habitual anger—is parental disunity. Often one parent will be in favor of maintaining strong standards of discipline, while the other will be more lax. Sometimes the parents may even switch roles from being permissive to being controlling and then back again. In families like these, the child soon realizes that he can't expect consistency from his parents, and a deep anger and mistrust may grow.

Consider how difficult such inconsistency would be for you. For example, what if speed limit laws were enforced inconsistently, depending on which patrolman was on duty? Very quickly, you would have no idea of how fast you can drive. And if you happened to get a ticket for going 60 miles per hour from one officer but not another, you'd be tempted to become angry and rebellious, wouldn't you?

In the same way, when parents are in disunity, it tells the child that the obedience one parent is expecting is unfair or mistaken and that there may or may not be consequences. The child assumes that there are no absolute moral standards; only one parent's grumpiness or expectations. It tells the child that at least one parent is wrong, and thus causes him to question authority in general and provokes him to anger.

Although rebellious children may learn to use the discord between their parents to their own advantage, playing one against the other, ultimately, the mere fact that disagreement exists between the parents will discourage and anger them. In some families, the battle between the parents about how to respond to a rebellious child is hotter than the battle between the parents and their rebellious child.

Moms frequently fall into this trap. Because they tend to be more tenderhearted—"Marshmallow Moms," as one mom calls herself—they might view their husband's discipline as severe or demanding. Even though a father may be overly tough, for the time being, mothers should present a consistently unified front to the children, and then, if she's concerned about her husband's parenting style, she can share her concerns with him in private.[2] If there's a real difference of opinion, both parents should seek out biblical counsel from a pastor or mature Christian friend who can help both parties see their areas of weakness.

In any case, it's vital that the parents support, honor, and respect each other in the sight of the children. In doing so, the child will learn that it isn't just Cranky Ol' Dad or Picky Mom who is expecting his compliance, but rather, God's established authority in his life. This isn't to say your child won't be angry with both of you at times. Your children will be angry with you when you cross their will, but at least they won't see one parent as more loving or understanding than the other, and hopefully, they'll learn that both parents are upholding absolutes that must be obeyed.

Failure to Recognize the Depth of Our Children's Natural Sinfulness

In light of the truth about our children's hearts—that they are born in sin and have a bent toward it, as we saw in chapter 1— we shouldn't be surprised when our children act in ungodly ways. We should remember instead that they're only acting according to their natures; their behavior is flowing out of their hearts (Mark 7:20-21). Rather than being concerned that our children learn to love themselves and have a good self-image, we need to teach them that "folly is bound up in the heart of a child"

(Proverbs 22:15) and they're unable to do right without the direct intervention of God's grace.

One mother we know reported that she found her two little boys, aged 5 and 3, on the living room floor, with the elder sitting on the younger's chest and hitting him in the face. As she pulled them apart, she admonished the older brother that he was sinning because he wasn't loving his brother. "I can't love my brother and be kind to him!" her son yelled in anger. Instead of saying what most of us would say—Yes, you can and you will!—she responded with godly wisdom: "I know you can't; that's why you need Jesus. He can change your heart and make you into a boy who can love his brother."

Do you see how this mother's understanding of the sinfulness of her children turned a distressing situation into a redemptive occasion? Our children can't be compliant and filled with wisdom no matter how old they are, unless the Lord changes their hearts. They need Him! She went ahead and lovingly disciplined her son, but the emphasis in this incident was where it should have been: on his need for a changed nature. When the focus is there, on the cross, we'll keep directing them to Jesus, the Heart-Changer, rather than simply trying to correct outward behavior. If we help our children see that they aren't "good" by nature, but are rather naturally bent toward sin, then they'll understand our need to discipline them and they won't be discouraged by their own struggle against sin in their hearts.

The book of Proverbs accurately describes the heart of a child who has not yet received the Lord:

- Foolish children (those acting according to their nature) disrespect and mistreat their parents (Proverbs 15:20; 30:11,17).

- A foolish child will justify his rebellion and sin (Proverbs 12:15; 28:24).

- Unwise children are self-centered and resist correction (Proverbs 17:10; 18:2).

- The heart of a foolish child is filled with anger, arguing and quarreling (Proverbs 12:16,18; 18:6; 20:3).

We parents must ask the Lord to help us see our children as they are. Within each of their hearts is great potential for foolishness, and unless the Lord intervenes, possibly through our faithful discipline, our children will live lives that will bring us great heartache.

As you look over the verses from Proverbs (including the ones in the questions on pages 157-58), stop and consider that this is the character of a child who has not yet known the work of the Holy Spirit. If this seems to be the heart of your child, let this propel you toward renewed prayer and faithful obedience, trusting that our God can change *any* heart. God can save your child's soul—He's able to save *anyone* who calls on Him in humble reliance.

The most loving thing you can do as a parent is to recognize the portrait that the Bible paints of an unsaved child's heart. This doesn't mean that we as parents must assume the worst about our children. But it does mean that we will recognize that the propensity to sin is woven into their hearts, and we have to be vigilant and wise as we fight the battle for their souls. "Look to the cross," we must tell them. "It's only there that you can find the grace and strength you need to overcome your sinful nature, and it's only there that you'll receive the power to do what is right."

Parental Neglect and Overall Busyness

One of the greatest areas of failure for us parents is selfish neglect, sometimes because we're just too busy. Instead of consistently disciplining our children when they violate God's standards, we tend to take action only when their disobedience disrupts our plans or desires. Can you imagine a soldier on the battlefield engaging the enemy only when he feels personally endangered or inconvenienced? When we discipline our children in this manner, we teach them that they can get away with anything so long as it doesn't discomfort us. It appears that King David was guilty of a similar neglect when he failed to take action against his son Amnon for raping his half-sister, Tamar (2 Samuel 13). Even though David loved God, neglect of his fatherly duties character-ized his normal parenting style with all his sons, as 1 Kings 1:6 reports: David "had *never at any time displeased* [one of his other sons] by asking, 'Why have you done thus and so?'" (emphasis added). David neglected his responsibility to discipline his sons, and he and his sons reaped serious consequences because of it. Did this happen because David was too busy with other pursuits?

Some of us get so wrapped up in our careers or hobbies that we fail to put adequate energy into our children's training. We know many parents who believe that neglect during the early years of their children's lives was a crucial ingredient in their later rebel-lion. As one parent told us, "I regret not being consistent in disci-plining my son. I had returned to college and was distracted by my own schoolwork. I regret not following through to see that he obeyed me. I would get busy and distracted, and then forget to check if he had done what I had asked him to do."

Another father now understands that the most significant factor that contributed to his son's rebellion was his absence from home during a critical time in his life. He now recognizes that he should have been willing to change careers so he could spend more time with his family. He recalled for us one particularly poignant moment when he was leaving for an extended period of time and his son, in obvious distress, said, "Dad, why are you leaving just when I need you the most?" This father goes on to remember, "As it turned out, it was during this difficult time of separation from my family that my son began his years of progressive rebellion."

Emotionally Distant Mothers and Fathers

Our physical presence is not all that our children need. It's possible for us to be together with our children yet be emotionally distant from them. When difficulties arise, we find it easy to simply retreat into self-protective positions behind the battle line and shield ourselves from further wounds. We need to be both physically and emotionally present with them.

How would you describe the quality of the relationship you have with your children? Does doing the laundry or closing a business deal take precedence over conversation in your home? We're not saying that you always have to drop everything to speak with your children; we're merely asking you to consider your lifestyle as a whole. Does the tyranny of the urgent squeeze out meaningful conversation? Do your children know what it's like to play and have fun with you? Do you intentionally have a night when it's just you and them, with all cell phones off and all email unread? Don't be fooled into thinking that you can have quality time with your children when you haven't spent any quantity of time with them. Relationships are built over days of seemingly unimportant talk and hours spent in little or no conversation at all. Quality time only happens in the context of ongoing relationship, not five minutes of interaction between television programs.

What does the Christian life look like to your children? Is it attractive, filled with joy and times of laughter, or is it only about discipline and duty? Believers are full of the Spirit's joy, and a common characteristic that we've seen in many successful families is that they make time to have fun together. When was the last time you asked your child what he wanted to do for fun and then went with him? Of course, some children don't want to do anything with their parents, or their choice of a fun outing would violate your standards, but what about spending an evening at a local coffee place sipping a Frappuccino together and trying to reconnect? It's worth a try, isn't it?

How many times have you commended your child today? Sometimes we tend to withhold any compliments or praise until our children do something really special. But we should be praising them as much as possible. That was the apostle Paul's attitude toward the Corinthians; over and over again, particularly at the beginning of his first letter to them, he thanked God for the work of grace he saw in their lives. The Corinthians weren't what we would call model believers, but Paul still found a way to highlight God's work in their lives, and we can do the same with our kids. Did your son refrain from an angry outburst when he was asked to take out the trash? Thank him and God for that. Did your daughter come home on time when her normal habit has been to push the curfew? Tell her that you're thankful that the Lord helped her be obedient. Praise your children when you see any glimmer of the work of God's Spirit in their lives.

Balance Between Expectations and Room for Growth

Parenting really is a balancing act, isn't it? While we've just encouraged you to be very involved in your children's lives (whether they want you there or not), now we're going to warn you about the pitfalls of being overly controlling! A parent who micromanages every little detail in his or her child's life will contribute to attitudes of anger and rebellion.

We know that it's easy for parents to demand obedience to unreasonable standards or personal preferences in the name of disciplining their children for the Lord. Although children should not to be completely free to make their own choices, parents must look for opportunities to respect their kids' growing maturity. Some of us would like to keep our children dependent upon us, small and trusting for the rest of their lives. But as godly parents, we must prepare our children for the time when they will be on their own. That means teaching them to make godly decisions and, when appropriate, allowing them to experience the consequences of wrong choices. The rate at which we "let go" is in proportion to their growing maturity and ability to make wise decisions. Many Christian parents provoke their young adults to anger by trying to exercise the same degree of control over their lives as they did when they were toddlers. Instead, let's strive to give our kids room to choose, to learn, to make mistakes, and to grow.

Now that we've examined some of the ways that we provoke our children to anger, we're ready to look at the second half of Ephesians 6:4: "bring them up in the discipline and instruction of the Lord." Because chapter 9 is all about discipline, we'll skip that topic for now and just focus on the "*instruction* of the Lord."

Consistently Train Your Children for the Lord

The Old Testament contains one of the most succinct yet challenging passages on childrearing:

> Hear, O Israel: The LORD our God, the LORD is one. You shall love the LORD your God with all your heart and with all your soul and with all your might. And these words that I command you today shall be on your heart. You shall teach them diligently to your children, and you shall talk of them when you sit in your house, and when you walk by the way, and when you lie down, and when you rise (Deuteronomy 6:4-7).

What components of soul-training do you see in those verses? As usual, God's first emphasis is on our motive, and our motive must always be love for Him. Any training we employ must have its genesis in love for Him rather than love for ourselves, our reputation, or even our children's souls. Training that springs from love for God will stand the test of hostility and discouragement and will be infused with humility and patience.

Parents Are Responsible for Their Children's Training

As we've said before, we parents are accountable to God for every aspect of our children's training. While we *can* use outside help in this process (just as homeschoolers use tutors and curriculum from outside sources), we can't delegate this responsibility to anyone else. The problems we face with our children are not ultimately the responsibility of the school we've chosen. God calls *us* to train our children, and whether we choose to keep them at home or send them to a private or public school, we must oversee their education out of love for the Lord, recognizing that all education is religious in nature.

Since our child's training is so clearly our responsibility, it is wise for us to think carefully about the perspectives that their teachers and textbooks promote. Do their messages reflect a love of biblical values and absolute truth? When they teach a foreign language or math, are they inculcating our children in a Christian, gospel-centered worldview, or are they merely communicating facts in a vacuum, not tied to any eternal truth? Training that is truly biblical helps children realize that God is sovereign over all the disciplines: history, science, math, language, music, and even athletics, and focuses on inviting our children to live godly lives and love His Word.

Is God's Word in Your Heart?

No one can communicate to someone else that which he doesn't possess. Your children know when you're being hypocritical, when you're fudging, or when you're letting your own life slide. Only when God's Word is on our hearts will we be able to convey it to our children with passion and sincerity. You can't fool the people with whom you live! If you want them to love God and His Word, then demonstrate this by being committed to it yourself. Have your children heard you pray? Have they heard you confess sin or worship God for His help? Are they aware of times when you've struggled with your own sin, and have they seen you go to God's Word for direction and strength? If you have a growing relationship with God, it will show in all that you do.

Teach Your Children the Word You Love

If we want our children to love the Word and order their lives around it, we'll have to spend time, both informally and formally, teaching it to them. Just as the parents in Israel were expected to teach their children God's great acts and perfect law, so we are called to do this with our children through structured times of family worship and through spontaneous occasions of sharing the precious truths you are learning from the Lord.

Although some children may balk at structured times of family worship, remember that the Lord commands you to train your children, no matter how they might respond. Fathers (and mothers, if fathers are absent or unwilling) should exercise their spiritual leadership by initiating family devotions, being creative and seeking to make the study interesting and practical for every member of the family.[3]

Just as God wanted the Israelite families to always remember their deliverance from Egypt (Deuteronomy 6:20-23), so we should teach our children about the redemption that God has provided for us in Christ. While we were slaves in the Egypt of our sin, God sent His Son to set us free from sin's penalty and power by dying in our place. Because of this great deliverance, we can now know true freedom and can live according to His Word, and in doing so, we'll be blessed (Deuteronomy 6:24).

Remember, even if your child is resistant to hearing you, you need to be loving and diligent in your obedience to the Lord. Don't let your children wear you out with their opposition. Instead, seek to consistently share truth with them, making sure that you're tailoring it in an age-appropriate and interesting way to their lives.

Persisting in the Battle

By now we've learned that we can't control our kids' minds and hearts. We can't force them into our dreams or recreate them in our image. All we can do is obediently follow the Lord and seek to be diligent to understand and train our children. Only God can touch their heart and transform their will. Of course this doesn't mean that we won't continue in the fight, using every avenue available to seek to impact them. While this is ultimately God's battle, we're called to shun despair and walk faithfully.

Perhaps after reading this chapter you can see ways in which you have failed (as each of the authors have!). If so, why not take time now to ask for God's forgiveness...and ask Him for renewed hope and diligence?

Dear Father,

You said that those who confess and forsake their sin will find mercy. I believe that You hear me today because of Your Son, and that You'll forgive my sin. I confess that I've...[list the ways that you've failed to faithfully parent your child. For instance, you might admit you've been afraid to carry out God's instruction because you didn't want to upset your children].

Thank You that You've given me the opportunity to come back to You again. I pray that You would forgive my sin and cleanse me. Please pour Your mercy out on me now, and help me to begin to obey You. I thank You that Your Son suffered for these sins and that You've already poured out on Him all Your holy anger. I also thank You that You now count me as righteous because of the holy life He lived in my place. Please do grant me the grace to humbly submit to Your guidance and cause me to be patient and filled with faith that You're going to accomplish all Your will in my life and in my children's lives. I ask all these things in the name of Your Son, Jesus Christ. Amen.

As you work through the questions below, remember that this battle is for more than peace, comfort, and outward obedience. We're battling for the souls of our children, and we're empowered to do so by our love for the Lord and His Spirit. We can persevere in love for them, teach them His Word, and pray for them with fervor because the Lord is the Lord of Hosts—He's a Mighty Warrior, and He is able to capture their souls for His kingdom.

Growing in Hope, Discovering His Help

1. Review the following proverbs to gain a clearer understanding of your child's heart: Proverbs 10:5; 10:23; 12:22; 26:6; 28:24; 29:5. What character traits in these verses (and the ones on pages 148-49) do you see in your children? What do these verses tell you about your child's heart?

2. What are some ways you have tempted your children to anger? What steps do you and your spouse (if you're married) need to take in order to correct the situation?

3. Proverbs 3:5-7 reads, "Trust in the LORD with all your heart, and do not lean on your own understanding. In all your ways acknowledge him, and he will make straight your paths. Be not wise in your own eyes; fear the LORD and turn away from evil." As you meditate on these verses, ask the Lord to help you see the ways in which you've failed to trust Him in regard to your children. In what ways can you lean on God's wisdom, and acknowledge Him in your parenting?

4. As you read the following proverbs, you'll see clearly that parents are to be the primary source of their children's instruction: Proverbs 1:8-10,15; 2:1; 3:1,21; 4:1,10,20; 5:1; 6:20-23; 23:15,19,26; 31:2. Have you personally embraced this role? Have you expected others, schools, and the church to take on some or all of this job? Are you aware of what your children are learning and what worldview they are developing? Would your children say that your love for God and His Word are paramount in your life? How long has it been since you communicated this to them? Ask the Lord to help you creatively think of ways to begin to do so today.

5. In four or five sentences, summarize what you've learned in this chapter, and share it with another parent.

9

The Discipline Offensive

We do not wrestle against flesh and blood,
but against the rulers, against the authorities,
against the cosmic powers over this present darkness,
against the spiritual forces of evil in the heavenly places.
—Ephesians 6:12

In the last chapter, we began to discuss the spiritual war that we're in as parents. We studied Paul's admonition to avoid provoking our children to wrath and we looked briefly at what it means to train our children. In this chapter, we're going to talk about discipline, the first of what will be a two-pronged offensive attack that you'll launch for the sake of your child's soul.

When Paul wrote about this spiritual war that we're in, he said that our fight wasn't against fellow Christians, but against "spiritual forces of evil in the heavenly places." Our warfare isn't against our children, either; but rather against those dark forces that would seek to steal and destroy their souls. As we wrestle with these forces, we need to see our children as territory we're fighting for—not people we're fighting against. We want to win them, but in order to do so, we'll have to wrestle against the power of evil.

God has given us an arsenal of weapons we can use in the course of carrying out our two-pronged attack: discipline and love.

The Need for Persistent Discipline

In the last chapter we considered the peril that our children are in: their hearts are woven through with foolishness. Their souls are not neutral territory, and it may be that our enemy holds sway over the territory of their hearts. Even though this is a terrifying thought, God hasn't left us without a weapon to drive the enemy out of the territory we love so much. The weapon? The "rod of discipline," according to Proverbs 22:15: "Folly is bound up in the heart of a child, but the rod of discipline drives it far from him."

In some ways, our children's hearts are like gardens. If we leave our garden free to grow as it likes, expressing itself without our intervention, we will reap a harvest of thorns and thistles instead of lovely tomatoes or roses. This is because both our gardens and our children's hearts have been affected by the fall (Genesis 3:18). God's Word tells us that a child cannot be allowed to simply grow as he likes, expressing his thoughts and behavior without our interference; as Proverbs 29:15 says: "The rod and reproof give wisdom, but a child left to himself brings shame to his mother." The sin in your child's heart is not merely silly indiscretions on the surface. No, sin is *bound up* in his heart, like a weed with deep roots.

As we begin to think about the process of godly discipline, don't fall into the trap of thinking that discipline is unloving or unkind. Although discipline can be wrongly carried out in anger or vengeance, *real* discipline is an outgrowth of true love; as Proverbs 13:24 says, "Whoever spares the rod hates his son, but he who loves him is diligent to discipline him." Even our heavenly Father, who loves us immeasurably, disciplines (see Hebrews 12:5-6). The Bible teaches us that the willingness to do the hard work of discipline is a test of parental love. Are you willing to love your children enough to discipline them, even when they might become angry with you? Willingness to obey God's commands and ignore the voices of secular parenting experts is also a test of your faith. Will you trust in the counsel of men, your feelings, or the revealed wisdom of God?

The Process of Discipline

What is biblical discipline? *Discipline is the process of setting clear standards for behavior based upon the Bible, requiring immediate and respectful obedience, and then taking measured disciplinary action when the rules are not obeyed.* Seems simple, doesn't it? Although it is simple to say, we know it's not simple to do. Applying biblical discipline requires work.

Before We Can Discipline Others, We Must Be Disciplined

Before we can ever hope to control a child, we must first be in subjection to God and in control of ourselves. The discipline of our children should resemble God's loving discipline of us. We are not to vent our wrath (Matthew 5:21-22) nor seek revenge (Romans 12:17-21), but rather to strive for the good of our children that they might learn righteousness.

Our Lord painted a very striking picture of what it's like for us to discipline others when we aren't disciplined ourselves. He said that it's like a blind person trying to pick a speck of dust out of another person's eye (Luke 6:41-42). The thought of that just makes your eyes water, doesn't it? The Lord spoke of the eye in His analogy because our eyes are so sensitive and so prone to injury. Can you imagine what it would feel like to have a blind person put his finger into your eye and try to fish out a little speck that he can't even see? That's what it's like when we discipline our child in ways that we don't embrace ourselves. No wonder they throw up their hands in confusion and frustration! It's so easy for us to justify ourselves on account of all of the sacrifices we've made. It's so easy to look at all the ways that she's failed and to compare ourselves and our righteousness to her sinfulness. But when we don't take the time to examine our own sin and to humbly confess it to the Lord and to others, we won't have the frame of heart that's needed to bring godly discipline and correction to our children. We'll be proud and demanding. We won't see all the ways that we've failed to serve the Lord, perhaps more seriously than our children. All we'll see is how they need to change and we'll proudly set about trying to change them without changing ourselves first. Then they'll throw their hands up in a defensive posture and resist us. Remember that God resists the proud (that's us sometimes, isn't it?), but gives grace to the humble.

Below is a list of some common failures of parents—failures that can blind us. Why not ask the Lord to help you see the log in your own eye before you try to get the speck out of your child's eye? You could underline the failures that are particularly significant to you, and we'll talk more about them in the questions at the end of this chapter.

- Have you been proud, failing to recognize your own sins against your children?

- Have you failed to confess your sins to them so that they can see what the gospel means in your life?

- Have you failed to spend time with them just for the fun of being with them?

- Have you been inconsistent in your discipline? Have you been too harsh?

- Have you called them names or maligned them?

- Have you neglected to monitor the influences in their lives?

- Have you taken time to listen to them or to be open to their correction?

- Have you been conditional in your love and acceptance of them?

- Have you been guilty of hypocrisy? Have you lied to them?

That's a pretty daunting set of questions, isn't it? Yet you can't administer godly discipline with a winsome heart of humility if you aren't willing to first get the log out of your own eye. As you do business with a holy God whose love was demonstrated in a big way on the cross, you'll be better equipped to offer hope and help to your child and to wage the war for his soul.

We Are to Discipline As God Disciplines

Even when we have to discipline our children, we must remember their weakness and our own struggles against our sinful nature. We are to deal with them patiently, just as God deals with us. Like God's wonderful work in our lives, our discipline is to be measured, using only as much as is needed to get the job done, and we must strive to avoid dealing with every minor infraction, but rather, choose our battles wisely. Think about the Lord's character and mercy in your life:

> The Lord is merciful and gracious, slow to anger and abounding in steadfast love....As a father shows compassion to his children, so the LORD shows compassion to those who fear him. For he knows our frame; he remembers that we are dust (Psalm 103:8,13-14).

Would someone who observes your parenting style say you are merciful, slow to anger, and abounding in love for your child? Would he be able to see compassion and understanding? The Lord does command us to discipline our children, but we must discipline as He does. How we need His mercy and help! Again, it's as we spend time looking into the mirror of the Bible and examining our own heart that we'll be equipped to offer this kind of love and mercy to our kids.

We're to Aim At Heart-Change[1]

Usually when we think of discipline, we think of spanking.[2] Measured, appropriate spanking is biblical, but we should remember that the true target of discipline is our child's heart. Merely controlling behavior without going deeper and speaking with the child about his or her heart is like merely mowing the weeds in our garden. Soon they will grow back, but this time with stronger roots. Chastisement should always be accompanied by a loving appeal to consider the heart, seeking to pull out the weeds of sin and rebellion, roots and all.

Spanking should always be carried out with prayer, discussion of God's law, and love, while reaffirming your loving acceptance of your child. If the child understands that you're endeavoring to obey God in the hope that the Lord will change his heart, then he will know that your discipline comes from a heart of love and concern rather than hatred, anger, or irritation. If we don't focus on our children's hearts, they will simply learn to outwardly conform to our desires while their hearts are filled with rebellion. Then when they're free from our control, their true nature will surface.

Take time now to consider the discipline you administer to your child:

- Are you consistent?

- Are you gracious and self-disciplined, or harsh and out of control?

- Do you ask heart-centered questions and refer your child to the Word of God, encouraging him to think about his heart?

- Do you reaffirm your love for him when you spank him?

- Does he know your discipline comes from a love for his soul?

Pray that the Lord will help you avoid the remorse of the father who said, "I regret being too passive. I also regret not talking to their hearts, but only addressing their behavior."

Protect the Borders of Your Child's Soul

There are many evil influences that can encroach on your child's soul and drag him into your enemy's territory. For instance, you may need to restrict your child from certain friends who have proven to be a bad influence. He should not be allowed to spend time with peers who are sexually immoral, who abuse substances, or who sneer at authority or break the law. Although you can't make your child become friends with godly people, you can and should keep him away from those who would seek to corrupt his life. You may, especially during a time of intense discipline in response to specific temptations, keep him under your direct supervision even when he is with his friends. As a formerly rebellious child wrote to us, "I wish my parents had kept me from bad friends and pulled me out of public school when I started getting into trouble."

If your child has been misusing the Internet, he may need to be completely restricted from using it. If you still want him to be able to use the computer for schoolwork, or similar activities, you could move it into a public place in the house and set up a security arrangement that prevents access without your help. We know that this might require a significant investment of time or trouble, but remember what you're fighting for: your child's very soul.

If telephone usage proves to be a problem, then restrict usage and prohibit long conversations in the privacy of her bedroom. You might even insist that all phone conversations are conducted in your presence so that you can monitor them—at least until she has re-earned your trust.

Of course, as we've said before, the music, television shows, films, books, magazines, and video games our children are exposed to can have a seriously harmful effect on their soul. You may need to block certain television stations[3] or even get rid of your cable service altogether. Even though all your child's friends may be watching certain programs or playing certain video games, remember that you're responsible only for *your* child's soul. If you think that what she's hearing is drawing her soul away from the Lord, then you have a right and obligation to stop its influence on her. Even the portrayal of sex outside marriage that's regularly offered up in movies with a PG rating can corrupt your child's morals. The apostle Paul admonished the Romans, "Do not be conformed to this world, but be transformed by the renewal of your mind, that by testing you may discern what is the will of God, what is good and acceptable and perfect" (12:2).

Is her mind being transformed, or is it being crammed into the world's mold? Later on in Romans, Paul wrote, "I want you to be wise as to what is good and innocent as to what is evil" (16:19). Is she wise about goodness but innocent about evil? Those are the questions you'll need to ask as you consider how far you'll need to restrict her interaction with modern media.

Setting Reasonable Expectations

Earlier, we spoke about how inconsistency provokes children to anger. It also undermines your authority. Because of this, and because our parenting is to be modeled after God's parenting of us, you'll need to be very clear about your expectations and the consequences that will happen when your rules aren't followed.

In the chart below you'll find a list of reasonable expectations along with a Bible verse you can use when you speak to your child about these new "battle time laws." We've also left a place for you to write out your own expectations and the consequences for non-compliance. Your child probably won't like the fact that you're seeking now to enforce these rules in his life, but hopefully, he will be thankful later.

Your Expectation	Bible Reference	Personalize It	Consequences
Curfew	1 Thessalonians 5:7	What time?	
Entertainment	Romans 13:14	What movies?	
Respectful speech and attitudes	Ephesians 6:4	What attitudes and speech are expected?	
Participation in worship	Joshua 24:15	Although you can't command belief, you can command attendance. What services will he attend?	
Treatment of Siblings	Matthew 7:12	What will your standards of behavior with siblings be?	
Substance abuse	Proverbs 20:1	Observance of all laws will be required at all times. The use of illegal substances will be cause for immediate discipline.	

Your Expectation	Bible Reference	Personalize It	Consequences
Diligence in school and work	Proverbs 6:6,9-11	What are your expectations for his grades? Are you in constant communication with his school?	
Contribution to the family	Proverbs 10:5	What are his chores? Is he to contribute financially to the family?	
Participation in family activities	Proverbs 1:8	When is he expected to be home?	
Dress and grooming	1 Timothy 2:9	What standards of grooming and modesty will you expect?	
Honesty	Ephesians 4:25	How will you check to make sure he's telling you the truth?	

We've placed the above chart in Appendix D so you can copy it and make changes to it as you see fit. It's very important for you to develop your rules according to God's Word. In doing so, you'll show your child how you rely on His guidance and you'll make it clear to your child that his problem with your rules are actually problems with the Lord's principles, not just with yours.

We purposely left the consequences column blank because you'll need to tailor your answers according to what you're willing to consistently accomplish. Empty threats will only serve to aggravate your child and undermine your authority. To help you, though, we've listed a number of suggested consequences below that you can use or adapt.

Remember that all discipline is to be measured out according to the disobedience. The punishment should not exceed what is appropriate for the wrongdoing. In other words, don't use a bazooka to kill a gnat. And once you've gone nuclear, you don't have many options left.

Your child should know, *in advance*, what your expectations are and what the consequences will be if he fails to comply. In this way, you'll teach him about God's dealing with our sin and failure and of his great need for God's grace. If you take the time to work through this chart with your spouse, you'll prevent yourself from over-reacting when you've had a bad day, or ignoring bad behavior when you're preoccupied or tired. If you're unable to determine whether your rules are too strict or your punishments not enough, why not ask your pastor or a mature Christian friend for their input? You'll need to be convinced that your expectations and the consequences for failure to meet them are just and good so that you'll be consistent in following through. Just as the Lord asks your child to obey and honor your rules, He's asking you to consistently follow through with loving discipline.

Clarifying Reasonable Consequences

Aside from spanking, which we've already discussed, you'll find a list below of consequences that can be constructive and effective. As you read through them, consider which ones might work best and when you might use them.

- Restrictions. Restrictions are best for acts of irresponsibility, such as bad grades or work left undone. You can keep your young person from telephone, video game, or television use. You can restrict use of the car (which should always be an earned privilege, not a right) or from visits to their friends' houses. Restrictions should be set for either a specific period of time, or privileges could be earned back through a consistent change in behavior.

- Labor. Extra chores can be an appropriate consequence for acts of disrespect. A child could be made to weed a garden, wash the dishes, or do the laundry. Since you'll have to make sure that the job is done properly, this might require some extra work on your part, so be sure that you're willing to invest in this effort before you set this as a consequence.

- Financial Consequences. Often parents compound problems with their kids by financing their rebellious lifestyle. Every dollar that you spend to pay for something (aside from basic food and clothing) should be seen as an earned privilege rather than a birthright. Please don't fall into the trap of thinking that you have to fund cars, insurance, expensive clothing, electronic gear, or entertainment. Your child will learn financial responsibility—and may be motivated toward obedience—if you tell him that these items (and others like them) will now be earned through compliance to rules and honest work. In any case, you are the one who is teaching your child about the value and use of finances, and he's got to see that disobedience has consequences.

- Restitution. Any young person who has caused a loss to others should be taught the biblical principle of restitution. For instance, if he is in trouble with the law for "tagging" a building, you should speak to the police about ways for him to restore the property. If she's run up a big long-distance phone bill, while you restrict her phone use, she can do chores or get a temporary job to pay the bill. Grasping the principle of restitution will be a blessing to her soul as she learns how Jesus Christ has made restitution for her sins and paid her debt on the cross.

As you've reviewed these methods of discipline, which ones seem most reasonable to you? How will you implement them with your child?[4]

Never Give Up with Your Children

When you first begin to impose these expectations and their consequences, don't be surprised if your child rebels and fights harder against you. You're in a war, and your enemy isn't going to let your child's soul go without a fight. You'll need to steel yourself to this reality, and through prayer and fasting, along with accountability to your spouse or a Christian friend, faithfully enter into the struggle.

As is the case with most wars, in some battles you'll know victory, and in others, you may experience defeat. There will be times when you'll think you've won the conflict, only to discover that your child has just gotten more clever at covert warfare. At other times, you'll wish that you could return to the "good old days" when it didn't seem like every day was a conflict. You might think that because you're doing what is right and trying to be consistent and kind, your child will respond favorably. But that might not happen for a while. This is war, and wars aren't won in one skirmish or even one extended campaign.

During World War II, Winston Churchill inspired the English people by his determination to never give up, no matter what the odds. The cost of defeat at the hands of Hitler and the Nazis would have been too great to bear. He said:

> We shall not flag nor fail. We shall go on to the end. We shall fight in France and on the seas and oceans; we shall fight with growing confidence and growing

strength in the air. We shall defend our island whatever the cost may be; we shall fight on the beaches,
landing grounds and fields, in streets and on the hills.
We shall never surrender...[5]

When you feel like surrendering, remember your Savior's per-
severance for you. Hebrews 12:1-3 says,

Since we are surrounded by so great a cloud of wit-
nesses, let us also lay aside every weight, and the sin
which clings so closely, and let us run with endurance
the race that is set before us, looking to Jesus, the
founder and perfecter of our faith, who for the joy that
was set before him endured the cross, despising the
shame, and is seated at the right hand of the throne of
God. Consider him who endured from sinners such
hostility against himself, so that you may not grow
weary or fainthearted.

Are you growing weary or fainthearted? If you aren't now, you
probably will be soon. When you're tempted to give up, remember
Jesus. He endured hostility against Himself from sinners. He
endured the cross and lived through the shame. Why? For us.
Because of what He's done for us, and specifically for you, if you're
His, you can run this race with endurance and shake off the chains
of doubt, fear, and discouragement. Why not ask Him to help you?

Growing in Hope, Discovering His Help

1. Ephesians 6:12 says that we are wrestling against evil powers. This word "wrestling" isn't a weak, pacifistic term, but rather one that means a "contest between two in which each endeavors to throw the other, and which is decided when the victor is able to hold his opponent down with his hand upon his neck. It is a term [that] is transferred to the Christian's struggle with the power of evil."[6] Do you see that your struggle against evil in your child's life is a duel with eternal consequences? Don't be deceived; your enemy doesn't want you to follow through with discipline, nor does he want you to win this fight. Why not write out a prayer for help and commitment in the space below, and then refer back to it when the battle rages hot?

2. We wrote that "discipline is the process of setting clear standards for behavior based upon the Bible, requiring immediate and respectful obedience, and then taking measured disciplinary action when the rules are not obeyed." Has this been your perspective on discipline? Where have you succeeded in applying loving discipline? Where have you failed?

3. Look back over the list of ways you may have failed on pages 162-163, 165. What points did you underline? Not only is it appropriate for you to seek forgiveness from your heavenly Father, it is also appropriate for you to ask for forgiveness from your children. Don't assume that confessing sin to your children will be harmful or will give them the upper hand. No matter how they respond, it's clear that the Bible teaches us to confess our sins (Proverbs 28:13; Luke 15:18-24) to one another in obedience to the Lord and in expectation of His blessing.

4. Turn to Appendix D and begin work on your Expectations and Consequences Chart. If at all possible, do this with your spouse. And if you need to enlist the help of others, please do so.

5. In three or four sentences, summarize what you've learned in this chapter.

10

The Love Offensive

*Love your enemies...so that you may be sons
of your Father who is in heaven.*
—MATTHEW 5:44-45

⟿

We know that one of the most difficult commands in all the Bible is found in the verse stated above: "love your enemies." *How can I do that?* you may be wondering. *Where can I find the power to cherish the ones who have caused me so much pain?*

These difficult questions have resonated in our hearts, too. And in this chapter, we'll continue to outline a plan you can implement as you seek to win your child for the Lord. In the last chapter we talked about one part of our two-pronged approach—discipline. Now we'll talk about the other part—love. As we make this distinction between love and discipline, please don't assume that there is a conflict between love and discipline, because there isn't. Love motivates our discipline, and our consistent discipline is a sign of love for God and our children. In a battle, sometimes leaflets spelling out concerns and hope for the citizens of a country are dropped instead of bombs. Both agents are useful, and both can accomplish a common goal. In calling this the "Love

Offensive,"[1] we're merely outlining another facet of the process of child-rearing that our Commander has called us to.

How Can You Love Your Enemy?

In the last chapter we said that we aren't really fighting our children; rather, we're fighting for their souls. We're fighting unseen evil forces, the lure of the world, and our children's propensity to sin. It is true that the world, our sinful nature, and the devil are our adversaries, but we're not called to love them. We're called to love *people*, and more specifically, those people who trouble and distress us.

Even though you might agree that your children aren't the real enemy, you still might *feel* like they are. When they scream at us or tell us that they hate us, it's hard to remember that they aren't our foe. When they reject your love or tell you that your Christianity is just a ruse inflicted on gullible, narrow-minded fools, it sure can feel like they're the enemy, can't it? So let's just assume, for the sake of argument, that they really are the enemy. But even so, Jesus' command still holds true. Even if they are on the other side of the battle from you, you're still commanded to love them! *But, how can I do that?* you may be wondering. As with everything else in the Christian life, the motivation and power to carry out the command doesn't come from you. It comes from God. Let's look at the words "love your enemies" again, but this time in their full context:

> I say to you, Love your enemies and pray for those who persecute you, so that you may be sons of your Father who is in heaven. For he makes his sun rise on the evil and on the good, and sends rain on the just and on the unjust (Matthew 5:44-45).

Jesus Christ is the one who said those words, and He's the only one who has ever consistently lived them out. He's the one who loved His enemies, laying down His life and taking their punishment on a cruel cross. He's the one who prayed for His persecutors, "Father, forgive them, for they know not what they do." God is the one who causes His resplendent sun to shine even on those who shake their fists at Him in the daylight, and He's the one who causes the rain to gently water crops that feed and sustain even those who blaspheme Him.

How can we love our enemies? By being what we are: God's children. Because we've been born of God, we have His Spirit residing in us. And in Romans 5:5, Paul points out that "God's love has been poured into our hearts through the Holy Spirit who has been given to us." The apostle John wrote, "We love because he first loved us" (1 John 4:19). We *can* love our children, but not because we're so loving or compassionate. We can love because His love is in us and we've been loved.

The fact God's love resides in us empowers us to offer that kind of love to others. What's more, we can love without expecting anything in return (Luke 6:35), and we can endure when it seems as though our hearts will break. How? By remembering how we've been loved by God—a love poured out upon us "even when we were dead in our trespasses" (Ephesians 2:5). You might be thinking, *That's easy for you to say! You haven't seen how ungrateful and evil my child is!* While it's true that we don't know your child, we do know humanity's heart. We were all ungrateful and evil, but God was kind to us! When it seems as though you've just spent your last drop of love and had it thrown back in your face, when it appears that your heart has been gleefully trampled under your child's feet, remember: "The LORD is good to all, and his mercy is over all that he has made" (Psalms 145:9). Because He's good to all—even to those who curse Him—we can be kind to our sons and daughters. We can love because we've been loved.

What does this love we're talking about look like? Does it mean that we just become passive and let our children walk all over us? By no means! This kind of love is active and intentional, seeking opportunities to bless, to be kind and merciful, and to open doors of communication. Let's take a few moments now to examine what this love looks like, remembering all the time that the motivation and power to love has to come from God alone.

Resist Revenge and Do Good

In Romans 12, Paul teaches us what one facet of love looks like:

> Repay no one evil for evil....Beloved, never avenge yourselves, but leave it to the wrath of God, for it is written, "Vengeance is mine, I will repay, says the Lord." To the contrary, "If your enemy is hungry, feed him; if he is thirsty, give him something to drink; for by so doing you will heap burning coals on his head." Do not be overcome by evil, but overcome evil with good (Romans 12:17,19-21).

It's easy to fall into the trap of "repaying evil for evil," isn't it? We're hurting and we're often tempted to deal with our pain by inflicting pain back upon others. Perhaps we seek to do this by becoming emotionally distant or cold. We might also become sinfully angry and seek to inflict reciprocal pain on our child through browbeating or even physical abuse. These kinds of actions are plainly sinful; they're not Christlike, and we're repaying evil for evil.

How are we to respond in the face of the evil or wrongdoing from our children? *We're to overcome their evil with good.* It's never proper to sin in response to another's sin against us. Rather, we're to ask the Lord to help us know how to respond in a way that pleases Him. And when we do implement corrective discipline, we need to be sure that we're doing so for the sake of our child's restoration—not because we have a thirst for revenge.

Romans 12:19-21 tells us how to overcome evil with good. We're to give our enemy what he needs. Does he need food? Feed him. Is he thirsty? Give him something to drink. Does your child need to know that you love him? Tell him. Does she need boundaries lovingly constructed for her good? Don't give up on her, but continue to rebuild all the borders that she's frantically tearing down.

There's an old saying, "Fight fire with fire," which, if you really think about it, doesn't make much sense. What would you think if you saw firefighters running into your burning home with flamethrowers? We would want them to bring hoses filled with water, wouldn't we? In the same way, we must fight the temptation to answer our children's sullenness with sullenness of our own, or to hurt them in the same way they've hurt us. God calls us to fight the fire of our children's rebellion with the water of unconditional love.

In the same way that a man might plot to harm his enemy, God wants us to make plans for the good of our sinful kids. He wants us to overcome their evil attitudes and actions by doing good for them. Again, this doesn't mean that we give them everything they want, such as unlimited money and freedom, because frequently what they want is self-destructive. Instead, we should find legitimate ways to heap burning coals of conviction on their heads so that they might be saved. We'll talk more about this in a moment.

Loving Your Child Unconditionally

We know that you wouldn't have spent the time it's taken to read this book if you didn't love your child. We know that you do.

In fact, you may be able to write down hundreds of ways that, through the years, you have proven to your child that you love him. Even so, your child may have convinced himself that you don't really love him, especially as he looks for reasons to justify his rebellion. Perhaps he's convinced that you care about what he's doing only because he's costing you money, or because you're worried about your reputation. In light of the fact that sin is very deceptive and we always look for reasons to vindicate our bad actions, you'll need to go out of your way to make sure your child knows you still love him. This is frequently the way that the Lord acts towards us, isn't it? So many times when it seems that He should discipline us or put us in our place, we find that He's blessed and encouraged us. Why? Because He wants us to know that His love never changes. It's in this same manner that you can love your child, and here are some ways you can bring assurance that you still care deeply.

- Keep telling her you love her. When was the last time you looked at her and said, "There's nothing you can do that will ever make me stop loving you"? Even though she might be unresponsive or hateful when you say this, try to make it a habit to communicate your love every day.

- Touch him with hugs and pats, if he will allow you. Sometimes teens don't want to be touched, but you might get away with a light hand on the shoulder, and it might be the only time he is touched in what he would see as a gentle way.

- Serve her favorite meals and have her favorite foods on hand. Most teens (aside from those caught up in anorexic behaviors) want to have plenty of food around, and you might even ask her if there is something in particular you can get for her that would please her. If she asks why you're doing this, just tell her it's because you love her.

- Open your home to his friends and show them hospitality by feeding them. Even though they might be rough around the edges, you can ask the Lord to help you see them as real people who need to know God's love. Try to get to know them and win their friendship. In doing so, you might find them siding with you in disputes and you may actually gain an ally.

- Offer praise whenever possible. Even wayward children— such as Absalom (2 Samuel 14:32) and Esau (Genesis 28:8-9)—crave the approval of their parents. It's a sad truth that many parents have embittered their children by being harsh, emotionally distant, and negative. We know that it isn't easy to find something praiseworthy in your rebellious child. Let us encourage you to sit down with your spouse, with a trusted friend, or one of your child's teachers and ask him to help you make a list of characteristics or skills you can commend your child for. Even if your child merely does a simple chore without complaining, that's something you can commend. Be sure to find opportunities every week to express your appreciation for him.

- Encourage any positive elements you can find in his life. While you might wish your child were devoted to Bible study and prayer, there are other wholesome activities that you can encourage her to pursue. For instance, if you've had to restrict the kind of music she listens to, why not ask her if she would like to start playing an instrument and offer to pay for her lessons? Perhaps she loves sports, and you could enroll her in extracurricular community activities such as dance or gymnastics. Just because you don't agree on some things doesn't mean that you can't find something to enjoy together.

Forgive As You've Been Forgiven

Again, all of our parenting is to be modeled after God's wonderful parenting of us. We're to love because we've been loved. We're to encourage because God continually encourages and comforts our hearts through His Spirit and the Word. And, we're to forgive as we've been forgiven, as Ephesians 4:32 says: "Be kind to one another, tenderhearted, forgiving one another, as God in Christ forgave you."

Forgiveness Is Always Possible

Your child may fear that he's gone so far that there's no way back. He might fear that if you really knew what was going on in his life, you would reject him completely. Because your forgiveness is to be based on the forgiveness that God has extended to you, and because God has promised that even the most wicked sin can be forgiven,[2] we can assure our children that there is nothing they can do that we won't forgive. Nor is there any sin they could commit that we can't see the possibility of committing ourselves and needing God's forgiveness. Why not determine that sometime this week you'll make it clear that no matter what he's done, you're always willing to forgive? Even more importantly, you can assure him that God is ready and willing to forgive whenever he might turn toward Him (Psalm 32:1-5 and 1 John 1:8-10), just as God was forgiving toward you.

If you're struggling with this concept of open forgiveness, you might benefit from remembering the ways you sinned against the Lord before He brought you to Himself. Your sins against God, the perfect Father, are far greater than your child's sins against you.

Even so, He's personally paid for your sins on the cross. His love and grace both compels and enables you to forgive those who have wronged you, and to walk in His footsteps.

Forgiveness Doesn't Always Mean Removal of Consequences

If your child is in trouble with the law or school authorities, you can freely forgive him while still holding him responsible to bear the punishment for his folly. You can assure him that your relationship is fully restored and that you'll stand with him as he learns the necessary lessons that are the result of his choices. Don't be duped into thinking that forgiveness necessarily means that consequences are eliminated. If your teen wrecked his car because he was driving irresponsibly, he may still have his license revoked or may need to make restitution. You can comfort him as he goes through the process of restoring what he's damaged. And, you can remind him that God's forgiveness *did* take care of the eternal consequences of his sin, that he will never bear these eternal consequences if he sincerely trusts in Him.

Communication: The Essential Element of Love

One of the most blessed characteristics of our God is that He communicates. You know, if He didn't purposely seek to reveal Himself to us, we would never be able to know or love Him. But Psalm 19:1-2 says, "The heavens declare the glory of God, and the sky above proclaims his handiwork. Day to day pours out speech, and night to night reveals knowledge."

God has graciously revealed Himself to us through creation, which testifies of His might and His wisdom, and through His Word, as Psalm 19:7-11 says: "The law of the LORD is perfect, reviving the soul; the testimony of the LORD is sure, making wise the simple."

Not only does God communicate with us, but He smiles on our communication with Him: "I cry aloud to God, aloud to God, and He will hear me" (Psalm 77:1). Think of that—the God of all creation hears us when we cry to Him! That's astonishing, isn't it?

In light of the open communication we have with our heavenly Father, we must strive to keep communication open with our children. How can we do this? Again, we've listed a number of suggested ways to do this. As you read on, remember what God's communication with us teaches us: *Relationship without communication is impossible.*

- Be very careful how you speak to your child, especially when he provokes you. Instead of lashing out at him and using destructive words, seek to use constructive, grace-filled words, speaking to Him as your Father has spoken to you. "Let no corrupting talk come out of your mouths, but only such as is good for building up, as fits the occasion, that it may give grace to those who hear" (Ephesians 4:29; see also Proverbs 12:18; 29:22).

- Listen. One of the big mistakes that we parents make is that we lecture our children without taking the time to try to understand them. When we're worried about the choices they're making, we tend to think that our words will change the circumstances—and sometimes that may be true. But we have to remember that true communication isn't a one-way street. Keep in mind that one reason your child may be attracted to questionable friends or even non-Christian teachers is because they treat him with respect and care about what he thinks. How long has it been since you sat down with your child and said, "I want to know what you're worried about," or "What matters most to you?" James 1:19 says that we're to be "quick to hear, slow to speak [and] slow to anger."

- Learn to draw your child out. Many angry children's hearts are like padlocked cells, and trying to figure out how to get them to talk can be a painstaking process. If you want him to open up to you, you'll need to make sure he feels safe and that he knows you'll love him no matter what he says. You may disagree with him, but you should always do so respectfully, remembering that he deserves respect because, sinful as he is, he's still created in the image of God. How good are you at asking questions? Do you care about his opinion? "The purpose in a man's heart is like deep water, but a man of understanding will draw it out" (Proverbs 20:5). Are you a man or woman of understanding?

- Spend time together. As we've said before, there's just no way to have an hour of "quality" time unless you're spending hours just being with your child. When you know that you're going to have time together, why not pray beforehand that the Lord will help you draw him out and understand something of his concerns? You might consider specific outings, such as camping or attending a ball game. Why not take her to the mall for shopping and lunch? Tell her that you want to be with her even if she doesn't feel like talking to you right now.

At one crucial stage with one of our sons, I took a day off from work and took my son out of school so that we could attend a golf tournament together. We didn't have any heavy conversations that day, but we did have fun together for the first time in over a year. I look back at that day as a crucial turning point in our relationship.

—Jim

- Remind her of happy family memories. You could talk
  about past good times you've had together when she par-
  ticipated in the spelling bee or had the lead role in the
  school play. You could reminisce with him about the funny
  sack races or that great family vacation you took together
  when he was younger. You could also ask him to help you
  sort through old photos and watch as he remembers the
  good times, and then trust that the Lord will use these
  memories to stir his heart.

Marshal Your Forces

Even though you may feel as if you're going through this trial
alone, you've actually got at least two very powerful allies at your
disposal: the first is prayer (which we've encouraged throughout
this book), and the second is the fellowship of other believers.

We know that as a Christian, you've probably spent countless
hours in prayer for your dear wayward child. Let us encourage
you to persevere. Although God rules sovereignly in our lives, He
has appointed prayer as one of the means whereby we might move
His hand. You might also decide that you're going to add fasting
to your prayer time, not as a magic formula to make a bargain
with the Lord, but rather as a means to humble your heart and
make you more dependent upon Him.

The other wonderful means of grace that God has provided is
most commonly found in the church. If you haven't already done
this, find one or two parents in your church with whom you can
join in mutual encouragement and prayer. Perhaps you can form
a group of parents who gather together weekly to pray for their
wayward kids, in much the same way that the mothers who belong
to Moms In Touch[3] pray for their schoolchildren. You may also
want to make friends with the parents of your child's friends, with
your child's teachers and even with law enforcement individuals

(if necessary). Even though some of these people or family members may not be believers, they may be able to reach your child when you can't. Perhaps a teacher or grandmother could speak to your child when your child simply won't listen to you. These people can be your ally in your fight for your child's soul, even though they might not see spiritual issues the same way you do.

War Means Sacrifice

Our prosperous generation knows little about sacrifice. Our parents' generation, however, grew up during World War II, at a time when food and fuel were rationed to support the war effort. The entire industrial might of America was devoted to doing battle against the Axis powers, and the people who helped knew what was at stake in this battle.

In the same way, you're now at a crucial stage in the battle for your child's soul. What would you be willing to pay or sacrifice to rescue your child? What amount of money would you spend, if it would truly help your daughter or son? What costs of time or career would you consider if it might be used by God to deliver your son? Are you willing to live without television or the Internet in your home? Are you willing to relocate your family?

We know these are hard questions because we've had to face them ourselves. But we also know there is great hope for you and your child as you persevere in this battle. The Lord is on your side—He's a Mighty Warrior, and He's also acquainted with suffering. Perhaps He is calling you to suffer with Him for a while. We know that's not easy. But we also know that He's faithful and will abundantly bless every effort you make for Him. Perhaps today will be your Victory Day. Perhaps the prayer you pray as you close this chapter will be the one you'll see Him answer. We don't know what His plans are, but we do know what He's like. He loves us even though we don't deserve His love, and He's always watching over us to protect, guide, sustain, and deliver us. Don't give up today, for you don't know what His plan of attack is, and when He will be the Victor. The one fact you can be assured of is that ultimately, no matter how we or our child responds, He will be victorious. Remember…

> The LORD your God is in your midst, a mighty one who will save; he will rejoice over you with gladness; he will quiet you by his love; he will exult over you with loud singing (Zephaniah 3:17).

Growing in Hope, Discovering His Help

1. What does Luke 6:27-36 teach you about your love and God's love?

2. Read Romans 12:17-21. What does this passage teach you about how you should treat your child? How would living according to this passage change the way you presently treat him or her?

3. How hard is it for your child to approach you and confess sin? Does he see you confessing *your* sin? Does he know that you're drinking deeply of grace yourself, or does he get the impression you think you're perfect?

4. Are you more prone to launch a discipline offensive or a love offensive? Ask your spouse which of these two areas you're weak in, and humbly receive this input. Ask the Lord to help you grow in both areas and to become more like the Lord, who disciplines because He loves.

5. Read Luke 18:1-8. Here, Jesus spoke on persevering prayer. What are the promises that He's making to you about prayer? How does this encourage you to continue to pray, even though it may seem that there's no change in sight?

6. In four or five sentences, summarize what you've learned from this chapter.

11

"This, Our Son, Is Stubborn and Rebellious"

He who is often reproved, yet stiffens his neck,
will suddenly be broken beyond healing.
—Proverbs 29:1

A s you've poured hours into the study of this book, we know that you've come through quite a journey with us. We trust that the Lord has used this book powerfully in your heart as you've faced the heartache that parenting has become for you. Up to now, you've learned to sort through responsibilities, your emotions, and how to protect your family. You've discovered how to watch for the evidences of salvation and behavioral problems in your children. With Laura you've sifted through the difficult maze of heart and body issues related to special children and giving your child medicine. And most recently, you've been encouraged to wage the war for your child's soul through consistent discipline, nurture, and love. It may be, though, that even after all this, you see that the situation with your child is more grave than we've

191

described. Perhaps you've begun to see him or her as completely out of control. If that's the case, this chapter is for you.

Look again at Proverbs 29:1: "He who is often reproved, yet stiffens his neck, will suddenly be broken beyond healing." That's a frightening verse, isn't it? As you consider your dear child, would you say that he's the sort of person described in the verse? Has all of the reproof that's been brought by numerous people—and all the love, nurture, and discipline—only seemed to harden him and make him worse? You know, although the pages of the Bible are filled with hope for even the greatest of sinners, they're also realistic about the fact that there are some people who just don't respond. And the Bible teaches that sometimes drastic measures must be taken for the sake of such a person, and for the sake of those whom he's hurting. For example:

> If a man has a stubborn and rebellious son who will not obey the voice of his father or the voice of his mother, and, though they discipline him, will not listen to them, then his father and his mother shall take hold of him and bring him out to the elders of his city at the gate of the place where he lives, and they shall say to the elders of his city, "This our son is stubborn and rebellious; he will not obey our voice; he is a glutton and a drunkard." Then all the men of the city shall stone him to death with stones. So you shall purge the evil from your midst, and all Israel will hear and fear (Deuteronomy 21:18-21).

This is another very disturbing passage, isn't it? Thankfully, we and our children now live under the New Covenant, a covenant that is marked with overwhelming grace, without which many of us wouldn't be here today. The remedy described above does not apply to us today. But still, it applied in ancient Israel, and it illustrates the seriousness of child rebellion. What can we, who are under the New Covenant, learn from such a passage?

An Incorrigible Child

The first lesson we learn from this passage is that there are indeed, and sadly, children who are beyond our help and incorrigible; children who are, *humanly speaking,* incurably bad or depraved. We say *humanly speaking* because we also know, according to the Bible, that with God, "all things are possible" (Mark 10:27). Although it might seem that your child is beyond all repair, God is able to save even the "chief of sinners" (see 1 Timothy 1:15), but for some children that won't happen until they've been completely broken and have suffered severely for their sin. We don't know whom God will draw to Himself, but we can judge whether our child is *beyond our help* at this point. We can judge in the same way that these Old Testament parents were told to judge: Does your child refuse to obey or listen to you, even though you consistently seek to discipline him?

Recognize the Seriousness of Your Decisions

You may be wondering whether your child could really be called "incorrigible" at this point. Because every child or teen seems rebellious and self-indulgent at times, we need to be extremely cautious about making a serious judgment such as this. It's not that you shouldn't make this kind of a judgment; in fact, after you read this chapter, you may decide that you will need to do just that. But we want to strongly caution you about the grave nature of such a decision.

Mutual Agreement Is Mandated

You'll notice that in Deuteronomy 21:18-21, *both* parents had to agree that the child was beyond help. *Both* parents had to have tried to work with him, and *both* parents had to bring him to the elders of the city, who had to decide whether or not the child was really "incorrigible." There had to be a mutual agreement between the primary caregivers in his life that there was no hope for change, and both of them had to make the decision to punish him.

The Authority in Your Life Has to Agree with Your Assessment

You'll notice that in Deuteronomy 21:18-21, the parents weren't allowed to take the child out and stone him themselves. The elders and the men of the city were approached with the problem. This important step was a necessary safeguard against the rashness of a parent who might be consumed by momentary anger or unrealistic expectations.

To help you determine where your child might be on the "continuum of rebellion," we've listed some characteristics of incorrigible children below. We're giving you this list *not* for you to brand your child as such. Rather, we want to *caution* you that sometimes parents say that their child is incorrigible when that's not the case. We want to help you avoid any possible serious errors in judgment. This evaluation should be made by more than one person; it's always best to involve both parents and others, such as pastors, biblical counselors, and other mature Christians.

- He consistently, and over a long season, has refused to follow your rules about household responsibilities, schoolwork, entertainment, activities, and choice of friends. He's living a life characterized by persistent and unceasing rebellious independence.

- She is angry and has frequent and ongoing disrespect for you and for other authority figures in her life. Her life is characterized by *constant stubbornness*.

- He incessantly blames you and your authority for the problems in his life; he is *persistently proud* and lacks any sign of true repentance or humility.

- She is involved in immorality, substance abuse, gang activity, or other illegal activities and staunchly refuses to stop; her life is marked by *constant sensuality and impurity.*

- He has harmed or seriously threatened other members of the family; is violent toward you; has habitually stolen from you; his life is filled with *ongoing hatred, strife, jealousy and fits of anger.*

- She's been involved for some time with the occult or with beliefs that glorify evil, darkness, or death; she's *thoroughly given herself to sorcery or idolatrous worship of wickedness or Satan.*[1]

As you read over the list above, what conclusions have you come to? We aren't saying that your child has to have every one of these problems in order to be considered beyond your help. What we are saying, though, is that if you can see your child clearly described here, you've probably lost control of him, and you'll need to take some pretty significant steps now toward correction.

Be Prepared to Take Drastic Measures

What are the appropriate steps to take with a seriously rebellious child?

Bring Him Before the Church Leaders for Discipline

If your child claims to be a Christian, he is accountable to your church leaders for his actions, as Hebrews 13:17 teaches: "Obey your leaders and submit to them, for they are keeping watch over your souls, as those who will have to give an account."

In the same way that an incorrigible child would be brought to the city elders under the Old Covenant, so a young person who is out of control today needs to be brought to your local church elders. As you initiate contact with them, you'll want to ask them to pray specifically for your family and to give you and your child counsel and direction. We recognize that your child may or may not be willing to accompany you to the church office, but even if he refuses, you can request that your elders come to your house to meet with your family.

As the elders spend time with your child and really get to know him, perhaps they'll be able to speak into his life in ways that are presently closed to you. It may also be that their assessment of your child will differ from yours, which will help you to avoid the mistake of judging him too harshly or of expecting him to acquiesce to certain unbiblical or unreasonable demands on your part.[2]

If you anticipate that your child will be resistant to such a meeting, you might want to communicate that you're open to correction and that you aren't just looking for the elders to be "hit men." You could say something like, "Johnny, I know that we've been having a lot of trouble lately, and I think that we need to get some help. I'm willing to have the pastor come and tell me where I'm failing to be the parent God is calling me to be. Would you be willing to tell him about your concerns and let him speak to you, too?"

Please don't look at this as a clever ploy to get your child into counseling. Instead, view it as an opportunity for you to learn and for your child to see that you're humble enough to admit that there may be significant problems with your parenting style. Most rebellious kids will jump at the chance to tell another adult about how their parents have failed, and you may uncover important clues about his perspectives. Perhaps at a second or third meeting you could disclose the problems you're having with your child, but this shouldn't be done in a "tattling" way, but rather, in humility and brokenness.

As your pastor or elder meets with you both, it may become apparent that they agree with your assessment of the situation. Certainly, if after time and encouragement to consent to a meeting, your child continues to refuse to speak to the pastor or attend a meeting with him, your pastor and the elders may then decide that the situation is grave enough to demand church discipline (Matthew 18:15-17; 1 Corinthians 5).

We know that some parents are reluctant to bring their child before their church leaders. Sometimes that's because they're afraid taking this kind of action will drive him farther away from the Lord and the family. Other parents are tempted by the desire to protect their family from the embarrassment of having their child's sin exposed. We know that what we're asking you to do may seem very hard, but we also know that although God's way does seem difficult, it is always best to trust God and obey His Word, as Proverbs 3:5-7 teaches:

> Trust in the LORD with all your heart, and do not lean on your own understanding. In all your ways acknowledge him, and he will make straight your paths. Be not wise in your own eyes....

Although God doesn't promise that our obedience will result in our child's ultimate repentance and salvation, God frequently does work through measures as drastic as church discipline to cause our child to take his sin seriously. We never know how God will use our obedience, but we can hope that, just as the immoral Corinthian man turned from his sinful life, so, too, our children might turn again to the Lord (2 Corinthians 2:6-10). Our hope is in the Lord.

Allow Him to Face Legal Consequences

Under the Old Covenant, the elders of the city weren't only the religious leaders, they were also the civic leaders. In our day, however, the religious leaders and the civil leaders are two separate groups. And just as you need to accept the counsel and correction of your elders, you also need to do the same with those who represent the state.

Unfortunately, in many circumstances, minors are not held accountable for their crimes, and the police are frustrated by a system that ties their hands. Frequently you won't be able to involve the police until your child actually commits a crime. Because of this, some teens learn to "work the system" in their favor and will scoff at your threat to bring in the authorities. If your child is breaking the law but hasn't been caught yet, you might have to wait until he *is* caught before you can involve the police.

If your child has indeed broken the law, he needs to experience the government required consequences for his actions. Sometimes parents foolishly protect their children from these results and actually fight against God, who has established government authorities for the punishment of evildoers (Romans 13:4).

Why do some parents resist the very authority that God has put into place to keep order? Usually because we can't stand to see our child suffer. This unwillingness to allow our child to experience the "benefits" of punishment may have marked our parenting style through the years. Parents who were too passive to discipline their children when they were young and could be easily corrected are usually unwilling to allow them to suffer the consequences of their actions, at a later age. The sad truth is that younger children who are brought up without "minor" discipline usually become worse over time and will end up suffering more "major" discipline later. While it may tear at your heart to implement discipline at a young age, you will be doing your child a great favor for when he becomes older.

Some parents feel guilty about the way that they've parented their wayward son or daughter and blame themselves for their current problems. While it may be true that you've failed to discipline and love your child as you should have, you don't compound the problem by failing to submit now to the authorities God has established.

Other parents are gullible and naively believe that a child is truly repentant simply because she's shed a few tears. Your children know very well how to "snow" you and influence you to get them out of trouble. Please believe us, as counselors and parents, when we say that young people who go unpunished for their crimes really do become hardened in their sin. They learn how to play you and the system and become experts in their rights and in evading responsibility. Although it is hard to let a child suffer the consequences of his wrong actions, it is loving to let him learn, and the sooner, the better.

Is It Time to Separate?

This is perhaps one of the most difficult questions parents struggle with. What if the struggle is so great that the matter of the child leaving home has been brought up?

Of course, some kids will leave your home before you want them to because they refuse to follow your rules. Frequently they'll find a sympathetic friend or relative who is offering them a better deal or more freedom with less responsibility. Or, it may be that they're so desperate for independence they're willing to live anywhere just to be rid of you.

If your child is still a minor, you can't just let him run away because you are still legally responsible for him.[3] Even though he may not be under your roof, you'll still have to maintain oversight over him, either by being aware of where he is and allowing him to stay there, or by sending him somewhere else. We know there may be circumstances that would prevent you from knowing his whereabouts, but you have to do everything you can to try to locate and watch over him, which includes notifying the proper authorities.

If your child is legally an adult, your options are very different. You cannot force an adult child to stay with you, even if you're convinced that he's not ready to be on his own. Sometimes the very best thing you can do is to let him go, even though you know he'll make mistakes, so that he can learn, just as the father of the Prodigal Son did (Luke 15:12-13). This parable demonstrates that the road home often leads through a far country and your child may finally grow up when he has to face the realities of taking care of himself on his own.

Putting Your Child Out of the Home

If your child is still a minor, you are required by law to provide food, clothing, and shelter for him. You aren't required to maintain his lifestyle, however. Because he's still a minor, you can impound his property (television, telephone, stereo, etc.) and restrict his access to money and cars. You are not required by law to provide a private room in your home for him, or even to let him live with your family. You can choose to move him somewhere else—with relatives, friends, or into special schools with programs that specialize in working with difficult kids.

Putting a Minor Child Out

We recognize that it may be your child has become so alienated from you that he might respond positively to a different situation. Before you send him out, however, be sure that those who are willing to take him know the nature of your problems with him, and that you agree with them and their life standards. It is fine for you to seek outside help, as long as you remember that you are still responsible before God and the state to oversee your child. In Appendix B we've outlined some of the options you have available as you consider where you might send your child.

Putting an Adult Child Out

If your child is an adult, then you can put him out of the house without fear of legal ramifications. If he is breaking the law or is a danger to you or other members of the family, you may even be forced to get a restraining order to keep him away. It is sad to think that you might have to change the locks to keep him out, but some parents have found such steps to be necessary. If your child refuses to work or works only sporadically, then give him notice of your intentions before you insist that he leave the home. That will force him to either find a way to sustain himself through a job or go hungry.

Some parents find themselves in the difficult situation of supporting an adult child who is in college or just starting out in his career and also living in complete rebellion. Remember that *you are not obligated to finance a rebellion against your own authority*, and we believe that it's foolish to do so. If your adult child wants to live independently of your authority, then he or she should also live independently of your resources. We know that this might be a very hard decision for you. You might think, *If I don't support her, she might drop out of school, or she might end up on the street.* She might even threaten to become a prostitute if you tell her that you're going to stop supporting her sinful lifestyle. But there are always other options for your son or daughter. They don't need to end up on the street; they can repent of their rebellion and humble themselves again under your authority. Even though your child is living away from you at college, you should still expect that he will live up to your expectations, including sending you his report cards, if he expects to receive financial support. Christian parents shouldn't finance four years of irresponsible living in a far country any more than they would support it under their own roof.

"But, That's So Hard!"

We know that what we've just told you to do may be one of the hardest steps you've ever had to take as a parent. Let us encourage you again to seek the counsel of your church leaders and others in your family, particularly your spouse, before you make a decision like this. Let us also direct you to the Lord, to plead with Him for the wisdom to know what you should do, and the grace to follow through.

You'll need to be very up-front with your child about the possibility of his having to leave the home and about where you're going to send him. Although you might need to force him physically into a particular program, it's usually best to give him a warning about where he's headed.[4] You can hope that just the thought of having to leave the family will be enough to turn him around. We know some cases in which this has happened.

Yet we've also seen cases in which children have continued to show contempt for their parents, and the parents have been forced to make this difficult decision. One teenage daughter who continued to beat up her younger siblings and file false police reports about her parents had to be sent away. Another teen son who was involved with gangs and drugs and stole from the family was put out. If your child is incorrigible and if you have other adults who are counseling you that it really is time for him to go, then you'll need to take this difficult step.

Once you've decided this is what you're going to do, you'll need to be prepared for how hard this will be. Your child may not go willingly, and the process of his discipline may even require having him handcuffed by security guards who will transfer him to his new home. At this point, many children will cry and rage against you. They will blame you for their problems and will plead with you for another chance. We're very aware of how gut-wrenching this process is, and because of that, we're warning you: *Be sure* that you're convinced that this is the right action and then stick to it, no matter how your child responds. As hard as it will be to send him away, it will be even harder to allow him to stay, especially if you relent this time.

Why You Should Send Him Away

The goal of such drastic measures is not revenge or even mere peace in the family. The goal is that the child would repent and find new life. You can always hope that your child will turn from his sin before it's too late.

A secondary goal is to protect the rest of the family (and even the broader church community) from a corrupting influence. Don't underestimate the defiling influence one sibling can have on another. The innocent children in your home must be protected from wrong or evil influences, even if that means that the child must be asked to leave the church and sent to live somewhere else. Although your prodigal may never return home in repentance, the rest of the family is still safer when he's gone. One mother told us, "When our son was in boarding school, we were finally able to focus on something else in our lives…we were finally able to start healing."

When Can He Come Home?

While your child is out of the home, take every opportunity to call, visit, or write to him. Assure him of your continued love by sending him cards and small gifts and tell him how happy you'll be when you're able to welcome him home again.

If you're like most parents, you'll be looking desperately for signs that it's time to bring your child home. Many kids who find themselves in a boarding school will beg and promise you anything to come home—and they know just what you'll want to hear. It's because of this that most programs have minimum-stay requirements that parents must agree to before they can send their child there. This is another one of those instances in which you'll need the wise help and counsel of others, particularly your spouse, mature Christian friend, or pastor.

In Search of True Repentance

The Bible clearly describes what true repentance looks like. This is what Paul wrote in 2 Corinthians 7:10-11:

> Godly grief produces a repentance that leads to salvation without regret, whereas worldly grief produces death. For see what earnestness this godly grief has produced in you, but also what eagerness to clear yourselves, what indignation, what fear, what longing, what zeal, what punishment! At every point you have proved yourselves innocent in the matter.

In the passage above, Paul warns us of a worldly sorrow that produces death. What does this worldly sorrow look like? At first blush, it might look like true repentance. Your child probably knows what you're longing to hear, and is undoubtedly skilled in using just the right words and intonations to get you to think that he's really changed. That's why we're telling you, right up front, to not believe every word he says about how he's changed. Wait, as the passage above says, to see if godly fruit is being produced in your child's life. This growth in godliness won't happen overnight or even in a few weeks, but will take time to be seen. Does your child continue to say the right words even when you tell him he's going to stay at the boarding school for the remainder of his high school education? Does she prove the earnestness of her faith by her humility when she learns that you're making restitution for her actions and she'll not have any spending money from you? These are the marks of true repentance, a repentance that is "without regret."

A biblical example of true repentance is seen in the speech of the prodigal son, who said, "Father, I have sinned against heaven and before you. I am not worthy to be called your son" (Luke 15:21). This repentant child's expectation was, "Treat me as one of your hired servants" (verse 19). If your child is genuinely repentant, he'll be willing to suffer the consequences of his actions, even if that means he remains estranged from the family for some time.

Your Hope in Grace

The hardship of living far away from home eventually led the prodigal son to repentance. While he was envying the food that the pigs ate (verse 16), he grew to appreciate the goodness of his father and his home. He wanted to go home, and he was willing to go as a servant. He had been changed by the difficulties he had experienced. This is your hope.

Parents should welcome and forgive children who are truly repentant, just as the father of the prodigal did. Listen to these precious words: "While he was still a long way off, his father saw him and felt compassion, and ran and embraced him." The prodigal son had done all he could do to shame his father. When he left home he asked for his inheritance, in effect saying, "I wish you were dead." But the father was willing to lay all of this aside and rush out to meet him and welcome him home. In the same way, we can hope that God will move upon the hearts of our dear wayward sons and daughters and that someday we'll be able to embrace them again and welcome them home. This is your hope.

Your hope is in God's ability to change even the most incorrigible child, and even though you might have to suffer now and take actions that are painful to carry out, you can still believe that God can turn your difficult circumstances into something for your good and His glory.

And, unlike the parents under the Old Covenant, you can encourage yourself by looking at the cross, where the sinless Son of God was crucified as a stubborn rebel. He's borne the sins of all His Father's rebellious children and He was executed in our place. It's this wonderful hope that you can cling to if you have to put your child out of your home.

Growing in Hope, Discovering His Help

1. Make an appointment with your pastor or elder. Ask your child to accompany you to visit with him, and allow your child the opportunity of telling him how he thinks you've failed as a parent. Rather than responding defensively, take his concerns to heart. Ask your child if he is willing to continue to meet with the pastor or elder so that you can work together through your problems. If he refuses to meet or if he meets once but won't come back again, then ask your church leaders for counsel about how you should proceed.

2. Romans 13:4 says that the police and civil authorities are God's servants, and that they are appointed to carry out God's wrath. If your child is in trouble with the law, how should you respond? How have you responded in the past? What can you do now to rectify any mistakes you've made?

3. If after much prayer, careful thought, and counsel from others you've decided that it might be time to put your child out, please get counsel from your pastor, a mature Christian friend, and the person in charge of the place where you're sending him. Ask these fellow believers to pray for you—that you'll be able to follow through, and that you'll have the grace to endure this tearing of the relationship.

4. If you're convinced that it's time for your child to go, you can refer to the list in Appendix B and begin to make inquiries about procedures, costs, and programs. Not all programs are good for every child, and certainly some programs are more Christ-centered than others. In any case, you may have to settle for a program that isn't quite what you'd like just so you can get some help.

5. In four or five sentences, summarize what you've learned in this chapter.

12

Your Great Hope

He will turn the hearts of the fathers to their children and the hearts of the children to their fathers...
—Malachi 4:6

The *GREYHOUND* had been thrashing about in the north Atlantic storm for over a week. Its canvas sails were ripped, and the wood on one side of the ship had been torn away and splintered. The sailors had little hope of survival, but they mechanically worked the pumps, trying to keep the vessel afloat. On the eleventh day of the storm, sailor John Newton was too exhausted to pump, so he was tied to the helm and tried to hold the ship to its course. From one o'clock until midnight he was at the helm.

With the storm raging fiercely, Newton had time to think. His life seemed as ruined and wrecked as the battered ship he was trying to steer through the storm. Since the age of eleven he had lived a life at sea. Sailors were not noted for the refinement of their manners, but Newton had a reputation for profanity, coarseness, and debauchery which even shocked many a sailor.

He was known as "The Great Blasphemer." He sank so low at one point that he was even a servant to slaves in Africa for a brief period. His mother had prayed he would become a minister and had early taught him the Scriptures and Isaac Watts' "Divine Songs for Children." Some of those early childhood teachings came to mind now. He remembered Proverbs 1:24-31, and in the midst of that storm, those verses seemed to confirm Newton in his despair: "Because I have called, and ye refused...ye have set at nought all my counsel, and would none of my reproof: I also laughed at your calamity; I will mock when your fear cometh: when your fear cometh as desolation, and your destruction cometh as a whirlwind; when distress and anguish come upon you. Then shall they call upon me, but I will not answer."

Newton had rejected his mother's teachings and had led other sailors into unbelief. Certainly he was beyond hope and beyond saving, even if the Scriptures were true. Yet, Newton's thoughts began to turn to Christ. He found a New Testament and began to read. Luke 11:13 seemed to assure him that God might still hear him: "If ye then, being evil, know how to give good gifts unto your children: how much more shall your heavenly Father give the Holy Spirit to them that ask him."

That day at the helm, March 21, 1748, was a day Newton remembered ever after, for "On that day the Lord sent from on high and delivered me out of deep waters." Many years later, as an old man, Newton wrote in his diary of March 21, 1805: "Not well able to write; but I endeavor to observe the return of this day with humiliation, prayer, and praise." Only God's amazing grace could and would take a rude, profane, slave-trading sailor and transform him into a child of God. Newton never ceased to stand in awe of God's work in his life.

Though Newton continued in his profession of sailing and slave-trading for a time, his life was transformed. He began a disciplined schedule of Bible study, prayer, and Christian reading and tried to be a Christian example to the sailors under his command. Philip Doddridge's *The Rise and Progress of Religion in the Soul* provided much spiritual comfort, and a fellow-Christian captain he met off the coast of Africa guided Newton further in his Christian faith.

Newton left slave-trading and took the job of tide surveyor at Liverpool, but he began to think he had been called to the ministry. His mother's prayers for her son were answered, and in 1764, at the age of thirty-nine, John Newton began forty-three years of preaching the Gospel of Christ.

For [his] Sunday evening services, Newton often composed a hymn which developed the lessons and Scripture for the evening. In 1779, two hundred and eighty of these were collected and combined with sixty-eight hymns by Newton's friend and parishioner, William Cowper, and published as the *Olney Hymns.* The most famous of all the *Olney Hymns,* "Faith's Review and Expectation," grew out of David's exclamation in 1 Chronicles 17:16-17. We know it today as "Amazing Grace."

Newton lived to be eighty-two years old and continued to preach and have an active ministry until beset by fading health in the last two or three years of his life. Even then, Newton never ceased to be amazed by God's grace and told his friends, "My memory is nearly gone; but I remember two things: That I am a great sinner, and that Christ is a great Savior."[1]

Amazing Grace: Still Amazing

As you read the story of John Newton, we hope that your heart was stirred to faith. Your heavenly Father is able to save the most wretched of sinners. He was able to save John Newton, the "Great Blasphemer," St. Augustine, whose early life was marked by intense self-gratification and immorality,[2] Martin Luther, who ran from God and pursued a career in the law, and He's able to save your child. Many of God's most faithful servants began as wild prodigals, including Franklin Graham, son of evangelist Billy Graham.[3]

We're sharing these examples with you because we want you to have hope. We know that as you've read this book, and as you've looked squarely at your child's life, it may seem like the easiest thing to do is to give up in despair. As you read onward, however, we believe you'll find help and hope for the journey ahead. And while it's good to know real-life examples of people who have turned to the Lord and been used mightily by Him, it's even better to have God's own word. This is the word of the God who said of Himself, "God is not man, that he should lie, or a son of man, that he should change his mind" (Numbers 23:19).

One significant aspect of John the Baptist's ministry, as he prepared the way for the upcoming mission of the Savior, was to turn the hearts of fathers and children to each other (Malachi 4:6). The Lord Jesus, who was sent to us, is the one who alone can change hearts through His Spirit. He's the One who can change the heart of your child. Although there is no absolute promise that your child will come to Him, God does give you promises on which you can fully set your hope. Over the next few pages, we'll look at those promises, but before we begin, why not take time to ask God to encourage your heart and then worship Him by singing *Amazing Grace,* which was penned by a man whose life was so vile that he shamed wretched sailors?

"All Things" Means "*All* Things"

Romans 8:28 proclaims, "We know that for those who love God all things work together for good, for those who are called according to His purpose." If you are a child of God through faith in Jesus Christ, you can be assured that God has a plan for your life and that it is the best of all possible plans. He is at work in your circumstances, even though it may not seem like it right now. The Lord, who promises that He never lies, is at work not just in the big problems or the pleasant events, but in *all* things. And He's at work for your good. Although you may feel as if He has deserted you and that there is no hope for the future, He promised in Hebrews 13:5-6 that "I will never leave you nor forsake you. So we can confidently say, 'The Lord is my helper; I will not fear; what can man do to me?'" Your enemy, Satan, may be telling you that your pain will never subside, that you should just throw in the towel, give up on the faith, and stop praying for your child. Let us encourage you to refuse to heed his lies. God *is* working for your good in this trial. On this truth you can utterly rely.

About now you might be wondering, *Just what do you mean when you say God is working for my good?* That's a legitimate question, and we'd like to help you find God's answer to it. First, it's important to realize that we frequently don't recognize the good that God is doing until years later. In fact, Isaiah said that God's understanding is unsearchable (Isaiah 40:28). It's not unusual for us to be blinded to spiritual realities because we see only a very small part of the puzzle. Just like Joseph, who didn't understand why God gave him a dream of exaltation and then sent him to prison, we probably won't understand what God is doing until later in the future, when we will be able to look back on our lives in hindsight. Joseph went through terrible times of trial when he was young, but in the end he was able to say to his brothers who had deeply wronged him, "As for you, you meant evil against me, but God meant it for good, to bring it about that many people should be kept alive, as they are today" (Genesis 50:20). For many years, Joseph could not see why God was allowing him to suffer. But after the passage of time and many changes in circumstances, Joseph was able to look back on his life and see that God had been putting a big plan into place—and that as a result of all that Joseph had gone through, God was able to make Joseph a ruler over Egypt, and preserve the lives of many people.

If you're God's child, what might seem like nothing but problems today are actually God's good blessings to you. God is using your trial to put you where He wants you and to make you a person that He can use in unique ways as He chooses. God's plans for you are good, and even though right now you might not be able to see how that could be true, you need to remember: He doesn't lie, and He's promised that this circumstance will eventuate in blessing in your life.

God Is Glorifying Himself

The greatest possible good of all goods is for God to glorify Himself. What that means is that through the trials you are experiencing, other people (and even the angels) are learning about how powerful, loving, merciful, and great God is. Now, you may be asking, *How has God already been exalted through what has happened?*

Sometimes God is glorified simply because you're continuing to walk with Him. Like Job, who didn't understand what God was doing in his life but continued to trust Him, your faithful walk is telling others (even your wayward child) that God is faithful and trustworthy, even in the midst of your trial. Real faith is "the assurance of things hoped for, the conviction of things not seen" (Hebrews 11:1). Even though you might not see how God is being glorified or how He's using your circumstances for your good, you're still trusting that He is doing so. That's real faith, and such faith brings God glory. It says that He's worthy of being trusted and that even though you don't see what you're hoping for, you know that He's right there, suffering with you.

Job didn't understand his circumstances, but he refused to curse God and give up. He hoped in his Redeemer, and that's what you can do, too. Job said, "I know that my Redeemer lives, and at the last he will stand upon the earth. And after my skin has been thus destroyed, yet in my flesh I shall see God" (19:25-26). Do you know that your Redeemer lives? Do you know that one day His rule over all things, including this sin-troubled world, will be personally seen by you? Do you anticipate the day you'll see Him face to face? This is your hope. He does live, He does rule, and you will see Him. Why not stop right now and speak to Him about this hope?

God Is Building You Up

Many parents who have gone through significant times of trial have told us that these were periods of unprecedented spiritual growth in their lives. That's as it should be, for James wrote, "Count it all joy, my brothers, when you meet trials of various kinds, for you know that the testing of your faith produces steadfastness. And let steadfastness have its full effect, that you may be perfect and complete, lacking in nothing" (1:2-4).

You're learning lessons about God's strength, mercy, and help—lessons you'd never learn if you weren't going through this. This testing of your faith will not cause you to fall away; instead, it will make your faith stronger. This testing will cause you to see the faithfulness of God to His promises and the profound ways His grace and mercy are at work in you. One parent wrote, "I'm so grateful to God that I've been able to see His faithfulness and that He is truly working all things in accordance with His eternal purposes." Think about those words: "I'm so *grateful....*" Are you grateful for your trial? Are you grateful for the work these trials are producing in your life? If not, you might want to pray, *Father, I know that I should be grateful for what You're doing in my life right now, but I have to admit that I'm not. Please help me by granting me the grace to see by faith that all Your works are good, and help me to want to be grateful now. Help me to remember all the ways that You've been kind to me, and cause me to see how Your Son suffered in my place. Please grant me a heart of thanksgiving.*

God desires to teach us spiritual lessons we could never learn by reading a book. The challenges we're going through right now with our wayward children expose our own sins and weaknesses and teach us humility and patience. Through these trials we see how proud we are, how we've relied on our own parenting skills, and how we're not really in control like we once thought. And through these trials, we learn to pray and to hope in God.

While these lessons are precious, they also hurt. With that in mind, you can pray, *Father, I know You're teaching me lessons that are for my benefit and for Your glory, but they really hurt. I choose now to trust that these painful lessons are meant to refine me and make me holy, so I pray that You'll help me to believe that's what You're doing. Help me to be patient and not try to "leave school" before You've finished teaching me. You're the Good Teacher: help me to be Your humble student.*

> Through this difficult trial, I learned that I didn't have the control over my children, or even over my own life that I once thought I did. I found myself in a place of utter helplessness and dependence on God. It's so easy to pray, "Give us today our daily bread," when our pantry is full. It's more challenging to trust God for food when you have no money or no job. In the same way, dealing with a troubled child has driven me to the end of myself and has forced me to look to God alone.
>
> —Jim

He's Teaching You to Trust Him

It's a truism that being a Christian means that we trust God, isn't it? Sometimes it seems easy to trust Him for the big issues, like our salvation, but when it comes to the day-to-day sequence of events, it's harder to see His good work. This trial you're in is meant to help you learn what real trust is all about. When we feel strong and in control, we can be fooled into thinking that we really do have great faith. But when the rug gets pulled out from under us, we discover what our faith is really made of. So our trials really do help to refine us and help us to learn that God really is trustworthy. If you're struggling with trusting God right now, you can pray, *Father, through this trial I've learned that many times when I thought I was trusting You I was really trusting in myself, in my own abilities to control and manipulate my child's heart, in my own plans and dreams. Please help me today to really learn what trusting You would look like. Help me to rest in the truth that You alone are trustworthy, and that You'll keep me safe through this entire trial.*

You're Learning About His Love

It is easy to love our children when they're sweet and they love us, isn't it? That kind of love is just part of what it means to be created in the image of God. Jesus taught that even unbelievers can love those who love them in return (Matthew 5:46-47). But when we're called to love a prodigal, we need something more than mere human love. We need God's love. We need the kind of love that God has bestowed upon us—the love He showed us while we were still sinners, while we were still His enemies (Romans 5:8,10).

One parent wrote to us, "Through these hard years with my son, God has given me a glimpse of the depth of His love. We're all wretched disobedient children, and yet God has loved us. My own love for my son is deep and my pain over his disobedience is great. Perhaps he doesn't deserve my love, but I now see how much more I haven't deserved God's love. And yet, He does love me—for He is love!"

You're Learning to Mourn with Those Who Mourn

There is a real fellowship among parents of prodigals. We are the parents who know about the pain of wayward children. We know about nights without sleep, the haunting doubts, the self-condemning accusations, the humbling abasement. We're also the parents who learn things we never thought we would learn. We've learned about rejection, disobedience, the drug culture, gross immorality, and violence. We've learned how to go to church and look at other families whose kids seem perfect and we've learned to smile and overlook their accusing stares. We may have even learned about the legal system. And just like the survivors of D-Day on the beaches of Normandy, we've made a connection with other parents just like us, and that connection makes us sympathetic and filled with the desire to comfort them. This suffering has brought us closer to family members and to our spouses because company is always welcome on the path that leads through the valley of the shadow of death. Many of us have learned, for the first time, what it really means to "weep with those who weep" (Romans 12:15).

If the authors of this book hadn't walked through these burdensome lessons, you wouldn't be holding this book in your hands. We wouldn't have had the motivation to comfort or help you, and our help wouldn't be what it is: help that's been distilled through the crushing of our own souls. Do you have compassion for other suffering parents? If so, God's work in you is bearing fruit. You could pray in this way: *Father, I thank You that You're transforming me into a conduit of Your love and comfort for other suffering parents. Even though this trial's been so hard, I do know that You're helping me to have love and compassion for others who are suffering like me. Help me to have the heart of my Savior, who went out after the lost sheep. Help me see other parents who are suffering, and may I seek to comfort them.*

God's Work in Your Child

Sometimes even when a child isn't brought to saving faith, God does restore relationships and open up the lines of communication. Although we as parents might remain very concerned about the spiritual condition of our children, we can rejoice when we see mutual love and trust growing. Frequently, as this relationship grows, we see our children asking for our counsel and becoming more open to the discussion of spiritual things. If your child is beginning to come around again, you can rejoice. Perhaps God will yet give you opportunity to see his or her soul saved.

You Can Hope Because Prodigals Do Return!

God does work in wayward kids. He's shown mercy to countless families. Just like John Newton and St. Augustine returned to the faith of their mothers, so your child may yet return. Many parents we've talked with have joyously told us stories of how their children have been transformed by God's power. One young man who had formerly been on drugs and who was kicked out of his parents' home when he was 18 is now a faithful Christian family man who works with troubled youth. Another man who was expelled from a Christian college is now serving God as a missionary overseas.

God has even used the sins of children to bring them back to Himself. One restored prodigal wrote to us, "I regret using drugs and breaking my parents' hearts. But when I look back now, I can see that these things happened for a reason. God used the bad I did for good in my life. He brought me closer to Him, and I found out how evil a person I really am and that I needed God's grace and mercy to change me. I discovered that going to church and being good in other peoples' eyes doesn't make me acceptable to God because God looks at the heart." This young man's testimony may be the testimony of your child someday.

"So Long As He Is Alive, Hope Remains"

Those are the words of a father who is still waiting, still hoping, still praying. No matter how far your child has gone, God can change his or her heart. God has been in the business of changing hearts for thousands of years, and it seems that just when the night has become the darkest and most hopeless, He comes in by His power and says, "Let there be light."

We want to leave you with two verses that you can pray for your dear child. These verses are promises that God made to His wayward son, Israel, and you can pray them for your child, too.

> I will sprinkle clean water on you, and you shall be
> clean from all your uncleannesses, and from all your

idols I will cleanse you. I will give you a new heart, and
a new spirit I will put within you. And I will remove
the heart of stone from your flesh and give you a heart
of flesh. And I will put my Spirit within you, and cause
you to walk in my statutes and be careful to obey my
rules (Ezekiel 36:25-27).

. . . I will put my law within them, and I will write it on
their hearts. And I will be their God, and they shall be
my people (Jeremiah 31:33).

Look again at those verses. God's promise to all those who
become His children is that He will completely cleanse them from
uncleanness and idolatry. He will give them a new heart and a
new spirit, and He will remove the heart of stone and give them
warm hearts of flesh. He will indwell them with His Spirit which
causes them to walk in obedience, and He will write His law
within them, on their hearts. He will be their God, and they will
be His children. These are the promises God has made to all those
who are to be His, and these are the promises you can pray over
your kids.

So…keep praying, keep believing, keep trusting and living for
Him. Let us encourage you one last time through this prayer you
can lift up to your heavenly Father.

*Father, You're the only One who can fulfill these
words. You're the only One who can cleanse my dear child
from sin. You're the only One who can give him a new
heart and a new spirit. Please do so, I pray. Please remove
that stony heart of his and give him a heart of flesh upon
which I pray You'll write Your law. Please motivate him
to walk in Your statutes and obey Your laws. Make Him
Your child, Lord. Please be his God, I pray.*

Father, I also pray that until I see this happen in his life, You would make me faithful and sustain me. Cause me to humbly submit to Your teaching and please help me see all the good blessings that this painful trial is bringing me. Help me to love and serve other sorrowing parents and to make my life a testimony of Your amazing ability to comfort and strengthen the suffering. I pray that I will learn to love You more and that my life will be more like the humble life of Your Son. My life, my children, my family, my testimony, and my future are all Yours, Lord. Let Your will be done in my life, whatever that might be, I pray. In the sweet and majestic name of Your Son who suffered so that I might be Yours, Amen.

Growing in Hope, Discovering His Help

1. Have you prayed the prayers in this chapter? What prayers can you add to them?

2. Take time right now to pray for other parents who are suffering like you are. Ask the Lord to use you to encourage them and to bring other faithful parents to them during their dark time. Perhaps you can form a "Good Kids, Bad Choices" group of parents in your church who will commit to praying for one another and being available to encourage each other.

3. What do you think God might be doing in your life through this trial? Write out the testimony of your belief in His good plan, and share it with another suffering parent.

4. What verses in this chapter meant the most to you? Why not write them out on index cards to have with you when your faith is assailed?

5. In three or four sentences, summarize the teaching of this chapter.

6. In three of four sentences, summarize how you have benefited most from this book.

Appendices

Appendix A

How You Can Know If You Are a Christian

W e are so glad that you decided to turn to this page, way in the back of this book—and there are two reasons why we feel this way.

First, the truths that are contained in this book will be impossible for you to understand and follow if you aren't a Christian, and we want you to know the joy of God-empowered change. But, that really isn't the most important reason we're glad that you decided to turn here.

We're also so pleased that you turned to this page because we long for you to know the joy of peace with God and to have the assurance that your sins are forgiven. You see, if you've never really come to the place in your life where God has opened your heart to the truth of His great love and sacrifice and your rebelliousness and your need for forgiveness, you must question whether you really are a Christian.

Many people attend church or try to live "good" lives. We certainly aren't as bad as we could be…and so we think that it doesn't really matter if we have trusted in Christ. If we're nice and we love people, God will accept us…right? You know, if it were up to us, if you had to live up to our standards, we might say that we're all okay. But, that wouldn't be the truth, and it isn't up to us. It's up to God…and His standards are different than ours. He says, "My thoughts are not your thoughts, neither are your ways my ways" (Isaiah 55:8).The truth is that God is perfectly holy. That means He never thinks or does anything that is inconsistent with His perfection. He is pure and without fault of any kind. That's not because He gets up every morning and says, "I'll try to be good today." No, by His nature He is good, and there's never a time when He isn't.

In addition to being perfectly holy, God is just. That means that He always sees that justice is served…or that those who deserve punishment will receive it in the end. Now, I know that it may not seem that way to you, looking at things like we do from an earthly perspective, but the Bible tells us that the Great Judge of all the earth will prevail. If God allowed people to get away with breaking His laws, then He wouldn't really be holy, would He?

In one sense, the truth of God's holiness and justice reassures us. The Hitlers of the world, even though they seemingly have escaped judgment here on earth, will stand before their Creator and will receive exactly what they deserve. But, in another sense, God's holiness and justice should make us all uncomfortable. That's because, even though we may not be as bad as we could be, we know that we all sin and God hates sin. Very simply speaking, *sin is any violation of God's perfect standards.* His standards are contained in the Bible and were summed up in the Ten Commandments in the Old Testament. Think for a moment about those commandments: Have you had any other gods in your life? Have you failed to reverence the Lord's Day and set it apart for Him? Have you always honored those in authority over you? Have you ever taken another's life or turned your back on someone who needed your protection? Have you ever desired someone who was not your spouse? Have you ever taken anything that wasn't yours to take? Have you ever told a lie or looked at something that someone else had and wanted it for yourself?

We're sure, if you're like us, that you'll say you've probably broken some or most of God's commands over the course of your life. And there will come a time when you, too, will stand before God's judgment seat. But don't despair. If you know that you are a sinner, then there is hope for you because not only is God holy and just, but He's also merciful.

God has mercy and pity on the lost. He has immense love for us and because of this, He made a way for you and me to come to Him. He did this without compromising His holiness and justice. You see, someone had to take the punishment for your sin. Someone had to die in your place. But, who could do this and still maintain God's justice?

Every person who has ever lived sinned and was therefore disqualified from taking someone else's punishment, because they deserved punishment of their own. Only one Man could take this punishment. Only one Man was perfectly sinless and completely undeserving of punishment. That Man was Jesus Christ. Jesus Christ was both God (making Him perfectly sinless) and man (making Him suitable as our "stand-in"). The Bible teaches that because of God's love for man, He sent His Son, Jesus Christ, to die in our place. On the cross, Jesus Christ took the punishment we deserved. Thus is God's justice served and His holiness upheld. That's why the Bible teaches that "while we were still sinners, Christ died for us" (Romans 5:8).

Perhaps as you are reading this you know that you are a sinner. You also believe that God is holy and just, and you are hoping that He is as merciful and loving as we've portrayed Him. What must you do? You must believe on Him. That means you must believe in these truths and you must ask God to forgive you of all your sins. You can do this through prayer. There aren't any special words that you must say. In fact, the Bible says that "everyone who calls upon the name of the Lord shall be saved" (Acts 2:21). You can pray to Him, asking Him to forgive your sin because of Jesus' sacrifice. You can ask Him to make you His own. The Bible says, "If we confess our sins, he is faithful and just to forgive us our sins and to cleanse us from all unrighteousness" (1 John 1:9). You can rest in His truthfulness.

Now, if you have become a Christian, you will want to live for Him in a way that pleases Him. In order to know how to do that, you must begin reading His Word. You should begin in the Gospel of John with the first chapter. As you read the Bible, pray that God will help you to understand it.

You should also find a good, Bible-believing church and start attending it. A Bible-believing church is one that believes in the Trinity (that the Father, the Son, and the Holy Spirit are equally One God), believes that salvation is entirely a free gift of God, practices prayer and holiness, and preaches from God's Word (without any other books added).

If you've become a Christian through the ministry of this book, we would love to know so that we can rejoice with you. Please write to us through the publisher: Harvest House Publishers, 990 Owen Loop North, Eugene, Oregon, 97402. May God's richest blessings be yours as you bow humbly before His throne!

Appendix B

Resources for More Help

⸺

In this section, you'll find organizations to contact, books to read, and find out about an organization that may be able to refer you to trained biblical counselors in your area.

Finding a Biblical Counselor in Your Area

If you need to find a trained biblical counselor in your area, please contact The National Association of Nouthetic Counselors at www.nanc.org or you may call (317) 337-9100. The counselors who are members of NANC will offer you biblically-based help, usually at no charge.

Teen Adolescent Placement Services

TAPS is a ministry that helps families of troubled and out-of-control teens. TAPS assists families in finding appropriate treatment for teens who have serious behavioral problems, abuse drugs or alcohol, or have school attendance and court/legal problems. Their services include parent support groups, adolescent counselors, short-term crisis centers, residential treatment centers, liaison with probation officers, drug and alcohol education, intervention coordination, acute care programs, schools, camps, and other alternatives. All of these services are at no charge to the families. TAPS also offers intervention transportation of adolescents to only preapproved behavior-modification schools. This service is the only service with a cost. TAPS transport agents are registered with the California Child Care Protection Trustline Registry. TAPS is recognized and utilized by many California Child Protective Services. Please call anytime day or night, 24 hours a day, at 1-866-411-TAPS, or 1-760-439-2087. The TAPS email address is taps14@juno.com.

The authors of this book would recommend the use of TAPS for crisis intervention and for help in making decisions about the placement of an incorrigible child. Any program or service they recommend should be investigated by you to determine if the methods used are in agreement with your perspectives and biblical counseling.

Lydia Home Association

This is a distinctively Christian residential facility for troubled boys ages 12-19. The clinical director is Dr. Gary Almy, and the home offers a strictly biblical counseling program that addresses behavioral problems and endeavors to get children back to their homes and to honoring their parents. The home charges for its services, and can be contacted at 4300 West Irving Park Road, Chicago, IL 60641-2825, (773) 736-1447.

Twelve Stones Ministries

This is a residential program of 10-14 days in length, and their purpose "is to return soul-care to the church by helping the hurting, training those who will walk alongside them, and encouraging both as they intentionally apply the life-changing Word of God." This ministry can be reached at 3610 Tara Court, Westfield,

IN 46074, (317) 670-0206, and their Web address is www.twelve stones.org.

Books to Read

Come Back Barbara by C. John Miller and Barbara Miller Juliani (Phillipsburg, NJ: P & R Publishing, 1997). A unique book in which a father and his daughter, writing alternate chapters, look back upon her time of rebellion and how God brought her to faith and her parents to a renewed walk with Him.

Age of Opportunity by Paul Tripp (Phillipsburg, NJ: P & R Publishing, 1997).

The Heart of Anger by Lou Priolo (Amityville, NY: Calvary Press, 1997).

Shepherding a Child's Heart by Tedd Tripp (Wapwallopen, PA: Shepherd Press, 1995).

Withhold Not Correction by Bruce Ray (Phillipsburg, NJ: P & R Publishing, 1978).

Rediscovering the Lost Treasure of Family Worship by Jerry Marcellino (Laurel, MS: Audubon Press, 1996).

Parenting without Perfection by David Seel, Jr. (Colorado Springs, CO: NavPress, 2000). This book does a good job of helping parents to understand our postmodern culture and how it influences our kids' outlook on life.

Overcoming Fear, Worry, and Anxiety by Elyse Fitzpatrick (Eugene, OR: Harvest House Publishers, 2001).

The Peacemaker by Ken Sande (Grand Rapids, MI: Baker Book House, 1991).

Peacemaking for Families by Ken Sande (Wheaton, IL: Tyndale House Publishers, 2001).

When God Weeps by Joni Eareckson Tada (Grand Rapids, MI: Zondervan, 1997).

Teach them Diligently by Lou Priolo (Woodruff, SC: Timeless Texts, 2000).

Proverbs for Parenting by Barbara Decker (Boise, ID: Lynne's Bookshelf, 1991).

Audiotape: "How to Help Out of Control Kids" (NANC Conference, 2003) by Jim Newheiser, available through SoundWord Ministries (www.soundword.com).

Appendix C

The Doctor Says My Child Needs Medicine

Should your child receive psychiatric medicines? Should he continue on the medicines he is taking? This appendix has been added to help you with this decision. After a brief introduction about the possible deleterious side effects of psychiatric medications in general, we'll look at the problems within each category of medicine, including stimulants, antidepressants, mood-stabilizing drugs, and antipsychotic medicines.[1] We'll finish with a summary that will pull the information together briefly for each challenge category.

As you read along, please keep in mind that you should never make decisions about your child's medical treatment on your own. All decisions related to the use of medication should always be made in consultation with a doctor.

Some Medicines May Permanently Change the Brain

Recent research suggests that some psychiatric medicines may stimulate the growth of nerve cells and new connections between nerve cells. Some of these changes may be permanent.[2] Because young children are developing new brain connections for the first time, a medicine taken during these years may have especially severe effects. Adolescence cannot be considered a safe time to give these drugs, either. Teen and young adult brains go through a second growth spurt. Because a child's brain is still actively developing until the early twenties, we should be very careful about using medicines that could affect this development.

Some of These Medicines May Be Habit-Forming

Dexedrine, Adderal, and Ritalin are stimulant medicines commonly prescribed to children diagnosed with attention problems. Stimulants have been known to produce serious drug abuse and dependence for a long time. Dexedrine and Adderal are closely related to the illegal stimulants crystal methamphetamine, crack, and cocaine. Ritalin is another related stimulant. Although your doctor may tell you that Ritalin is less likely to be abused than the others, Ritalin abuse is not uncommon among teenagers. It has been banned in Sweden since the 1960s for this reason. There have even been reports of Ritalin being dissolved in water and injected by drug abusers.[3] The Food and Drug Administration (FDA) classifies all three of these drugs as controlled substances. This tells us that, by definition, they all have serious potential for drug abuse.

The newer antidepressants are described as "stimulating" antidepressants because their effects are similar in many ways to those of the stimulants. The *Physician's Desk Reference* (PDR) lists "withdrawal syndrome" as one of the problems seen during the clinical trials of some of these drugs.[4] This means that some people have difficulty when they try to stop taking them, even though these drugs are currently not classified as habit-forming.

At least two other classes of drugs, Valium-type tranquilizers and stimulants, were first advertised many years ago as not being habit-forming. Later it became clear that they were. The FDA now classifies them as controlled substances. We don't know whether this will also happen with the new antidepressants, but this is a serious consideration for every parent.[5]

Some Medicines May Not Be Safe or Effective in Children

Although Ritalin, Dexedrine, and the active agents in Adderal have been in use for many years, there have been no studies about the long-term effects of these medicines. Illegal stimulant drugs like cocaine, methamphetamine, and ecstasy, which are very similar to these legal stimulant drugs, are known to produce brain damage with regular or abusive use.

The stimulating effects of the newer antidepressants have caused Dr. Joseph Glenmullen, professor of psychiatry at Harvard Medical School, to suggest that their long-term effects may also be similar to the effects of illegal stimulant drugs.[6] What is disturbing is that no one can really answer the question of whether stimulants or the new antidepressants are dangerous over the long term to children, or even to adults.

There have been questions raised about the short-term safeness of the new antidepressants, as well. The British Committee on the Safety of Medicine (CSM) reported that none of the new antidepressants but Prozac has been determined to be effective in children with depression. The CSM advised British doctors not to prescribe any of these drugs but Prozac to depressed children because the benefit of using them does not outweigh the risks of suicide and violent behavior.[7] It should be emphasized that the CSM did not find Prozac to be safer than the other new antidepressants—only that it was effective for depression in children. It found the other antidepressants to be *neither* effective nor safe.

Like the CSM, the FDA has found only Prozac to be effective for the treatment of depression in children. On September 14, 2004, the FDA committee studying the question of the safety of antidepressant treatment in children concluded that all the new antidepressants, including Prozac, cause an increase in suicidal thoughts.[8]

The *New York Times* quoted a physician present at this recent meeting:

> "We have very good evidence of harm and very little evidence of efficacy," said Dr. Thomas Newman, a professor of epidemiology and pediatrics at the University of California, San Francisco. "It would not be that bad if the use of these drugs declined, because it's very unclear that they work."[9]

These drugs have limited effectiveness and serious safety concerns when used in children. A doctor wanting to prescribe one of these drugs for your child should be prepared to explain why he thinks they are safe in the face of this evidence.

There are also safety concerns about the use of antipsychotic and mood-stabilizing drugs. The safeness and effectiveness of antipsychotic drugs in children has not been established. Most medicines that are used as mood stabilizers have been tested for safeness and effectiveness in the treatment of epilepsy in children. But none of them have been tested for safeness and effectiveness in the treatment of mania in children. Lithium, also sometimes prescribed to children, has only been tested in children over age 12 for the treatment of mania. But it is a dangerous drug, even for adults.

Side Effects of Specific Psychiatric Medicines

This section lists the side effects of psychiatric medicines according to their basic drug class: stimulant, antidepressant, mood stabilizer, or antipsychotic. Children with academic/behavioral challenges are commonly prescribed stimulants. Children with anxiety/habit and emotional challenges are prescribed antidepressants and mood stabilizers. Children with cognitive-perceptual challenges are prescribed antipsychotic medicines. Children with TBI (Traumatic Brain Injury) and developmental challenges can receive a variety of medicines, depending upon their symptoms.

Stimulants

The most serious risks of stimulant medicines are mania (a seriously hyperactive condition), and psychosis (crazy thoughts and behavior). They are also reported to both produce and worsen tics (frequent muscle spasms). Children with many tics are often diagnosed with Tourette's syndrome.

Probably the most common effect of stimulants is loss of appetite. This is why these medicines were first sold as diet pills in the 1950s. Stimulants may stunt the growth of children. They also commonly cause nervousness, sleeplessness, and irritability. Stimulants can elevate a child's blood pressure and heart rate, and have been associated rarely with heart and liver failure.

Antidepressants

The newer antidepressants were initially advertised as safer alternatives to older antidepressants, which were rarely used in children. But we now know that they can produce seizures, mania, and psychosis, just as the older drugs did. The FDA has also warned physicians that anxiety, agitation, panic attacks, insomnia, irritability, hostility, impulsivity, akathisia (severe restlessness), hypomania, and mania are associated with the use of these antidepressants.[10]

Extrapyramidal symptoms (EPS) are potentially serious effects of these medicines.[11] These include akathisia (an agonizing inner restlessness), dyskinesia (involuntary movements of the body), dystonia (involuntary muscle spasms), and drug-induced Parkinson's syndrome. Some doctors believe that akathisia may be behind the irritability, aggression, and suicidal thoughts that some children develop on these medicines. It's a sad note that a number of "school shooter" teens were on these antidepressants at the time they committed their murders.

Tardive dyskinesia (TD), a dreaded side effect, produces involuntary movements that may be *permanent*. There is no cure for TD.

Appetite is often poor at the beginning of treatment with these drugs, but later, a weight gain of 20 pounds or more is common. These drugs can also cause anxiety, depression, and sleeplessness. Although they are prescribed for anxiety and depression, they can make these problems worse.

Strattera is a new drug for attention problems. I mention it here because although it is advertised as a nonstimulant treatment for ADHD, it is similar to other new antidepressants. Many parents who are uncomfortable with the side effects of stimulants are offered Strattera as an alternative for their children.

Strattera was developed as an antidepressant, but was put on the market for attention problems after doctors began using antidepressants on kids diagnosed with ADHD who did not do well on stimulants.[12] Because Strattera is still relatively new, there is not a lot of information on adverse effects available yet. It is safest to view it as another new antidepressant rather than as a "safer Ritalin" until more information is available.

Known side effects include impairment of growth, increased blood pressure, aggression, irritability, difficulty sleeping, mood swings, and depression. A recent clinical trial determined that Strattera is not as effective as Concerta, which is a slow-release version of Ritalin.[13] Strattera has not been tested in children under age six.

Mood-Stabilizing Drugs

Lithium is prescribed for unstable moods. It can produce all of the extrapyramidal symptoms (EPS) described in the section on antidepressants. People taking lithium commonly complain of shaking, confusion, mental slowing, and memory problems. Serious kidney, heart, and thyroid problems have been associated with lithium use. It can also cause hair loss, weight gain, and acne.

The toxic level of lithium is nearly the same as the therapeutic level. This means that people can experience toxic effects even when their blood levels are within the proper range. People on lithium get frequent blood tests to check their lithium levels, but there is no guarantee that if the blood level is right there will be no toxicity. Lithium toxicity can produce kidney damage, coma, and brain damage.

Medicines used to treat epilepsy are also used to treat unstable moods. The most common one used with children is Depakote. Depakote can cause life-threatening liver damage and pancreatitis, low blood platelet levels, and high blood ammonia levels. Platelets are necessary for clotting the blood, and ammonia at high levels can lead to coma and death. These side effects can be very serious. Nausea, sleepiness, dizziness, and weakness are also frequent effects.

Antipsychotic Drugs

Antipsychotic drugs are used to treat "crazy" thoughts and behavior. There are two basic groups of antipsychotic drugs. The older drugs produce a very high rate of EPS, as described in the section on antidepressants. These include Haldol and Prolixin. They are rarely used any more, even in adults. Children normally receive the newer drugs, such as Zyprexa and Risperdal.

The most serious side effect your child can get from antipsychotic drugs is tardive dyskinesia (TD). A person with TD can have permanent involuntary movements, particularly of the face and neck. These movements can include an uncontrollable sticking out of the tongue and grimacing. The older antipsychotic drugs have high rates of TD with long-term use.

The new antipsychotics have not been in use long enough for us to know if they will produce such high rates of TD. Those who have had episodes of EPS are at higher risk for TD, and the newer antipsychotics produce less EPS. So probably the risk for TD over time with these newer drugs will be lower than with the older antipsychotics.

Another problem with the newer antipsychotics is uncontrolled, and sometimes massive, weight gain over time. This weight gain increases the risk of diabetes in people who take these drugs. A third possible side effect is neuroleptic malignant syndrome (NMS). This is a rare complication that can lead to death.

Other common side effects include sleepiness, low blood pressure, fainting, and seizures. Girls can stop having menstrual periods, and boys can have breast development due to a hormone that these medicines elevate. There can also be liver damage and an inability to tolerate hot weather that can be quite serious.

Should Your Child Take Psychiatric Medicines?

All of these drugs could cause serious problems in your child. Should you ever accept this risk? You might consider it if the possible benefit outweighs the risk, especially if there is no good alternative to the use of medicine. But as we noted in chapter 7, in many cases, there are good alternatives.

For example, an inattentive child can learn to pay attention. Children who do not learn to pay attention may grow into inattentive adults who may end up continuing to receive stimulants. Stimulants can stunt growth and can be habit-forming. They can also be abused. Some children and adults who take them will develop mania and end up receiving more drugs. There are nonmedical alternatives to drugs used to treat academic and behavioral challenges.

Antidepressants given for anxiety can increase the physical symptoms of anxiety. They may produce even more anxiety when usage is suddenly stopped, and some people even find that they cannot stop taking them. These drugs can produce mania, violence, and suicidal feelings, particularly in children.

Over time, the same dosage can fail to control symptoms, so the dosage may need to be increased, or more drugs may be required to achieve the same results. This increases the risk of side effects, which may be mistaken for new symptoms that need treatment.

Antidepressants prescribed for emotional challenges can produce the same problems. With the exception of Prozac, the antidepressants currently in use have not demonstrated effectiveness against depression in children and teenagers. On the other hand, they can produce mania, violence, and suicidal feelings. Prozac, although seemingly more effective, is no safer than any of the other drugs. If your child has entertained suicidal thoughts, there is a very real possibility that drug treatment may make him worse rather than save his life.

If your child has developed mania, he may need to take mood-stabilizing drugs, at least for a time, for this serious condition. The mood stabilizers that are used to treat epilepsy are safer than lithium, although they also can produce serious side effects. Although the FDA recently approved some antipsychotics to treat mania without an additional mood stabilizer, the anti-epilepsy drugs are a safer choice for a one-drug treatment.

If your child is severely out of touch with reality as well as manic, he may receive an antipsychotic drug along with the mood stabilizer for a time. In this case, the sooner the antipsychotic can be discontinued, the better. A recent study showed that people maintained on an antipsychotic along with their mood stabilizer after their manic episode resolves tend to develop depression.[14]

Bipolar disorder has become commonly diagnosed in teens with strong mood swings without mania. These teens often receive both antidepressants and mood stabilizers. Parents of these "bipolar" kids should remember that proof of the effectiveness of this treatment for mood swings is scant, and antidepressant treatment can be dangerous.

Therapeutic Tail-Chasing

When it comes to using medication for the treatment of various problems, there is a very real danger of therapeutic tail-chasing. Antidepressants prescribed for depression can increase irritability. So, mood stabilizers are then given to treat a supposed bipolar disorder. Since mood stabilizers can produce depression, either an increase in antidepressant dosage or adding a third drug is the next step in this cycle. And so on and so on. In most cases of anxiety and emotional instability, there are nonmedical alternatives to drug treatment which, when consistently practiced, will help you avoid this tail-chasing.

Because tics and EPS are well-known side effects of many psychiatric medicines, a child who has been diagnosed with Tourette's syndrome since beginning any of these drugs should be taken off of them first. Although many kids with tics just have a nervous habit that will respond to the interventions discussed in chapter 7, if your child is already on medicine, he may have a true involuntary movement problem brought on by the medicine. More medicine may suppress the movements produced by a first medicine, but at the cost of still more side effects, or even permanent brain damage. This is known to happen in persons with TD who are given more medicine to supress their abnormal movements.

When Drug Treatment May Be Necessary

Children with cognitive-perceptual challenges face a difficult dilemma. The primary drugs used to treat these challenges are the antipsychotics, which can produce TD, NMS, serious obesity, and diabetes. But a child who is hallucinating and has delusions (believes "crazy" things) can be a serious danger to himself and others. Parents will need to seriously weigh the dangers of these drugs against the danger that the child may be to himself or to others.

Children with severe developmental disabilities and TBI may also be a danger to themselves or others without medicine to help control their behavior. These medicines may include antipsychotics and mood stabilizers.

In all cases where antipsychotic medicines are used, effort should be made to use *the lowest dosage for the shortest time possible* because TD and diabetes can develop with long-term treatment. In spite of the dangers, however, these medicines can be life-saving when used carefully in the case of cognitive-perceptual and developmental challenges.

Finding the Best Doctor for Your Child

A parent who decides after prayerful consideration to use any of these drugs should make sure that the doctor treating his child is an expert in their use. Family practitioners and pediatricians often prescribe stimulants and antidepressants, but child psychiatrists are experts in the use of these drugs in children. Only a psychiatrist should prescribe antipsychotic medicines.

A child with developmental challenges should be under the care of a child psychiatrist who is an expert in developmental issues, or a developmental neurologist. A child with TBI should be under the care of a child psychiatrist or child neurologist who is experienced in the treatment of traumatic brain injury. To be sure that he is competent, you should choose a doctor who is board-certified in his area of specialty.

If You Would Like Your Child to Stop His Medicines

If you decide that you would like your child to stop taking psychiatric medicines, we urge you to do this under the supervision of a doctor. If your child has been receiving his medicines from your family doctor or pediatrician, you might consider seeking a second opinion from a specialist, as mentioned earlier. You can tell this doctor that you would like to take your child off the medicines, and he will work with you to do so safely. This is important because stopping some medicines suddenly can produce distressing physical symptoms, including an increase in the symptoms that the medicines were given to treat. This does not necessarily mean your child needs to continue the medicine. He may just need to have the dosage decreased slowly. Movement disorders such as TD can also emerge as medicine is withdrawn. A specialist who understands these possible reactions can help your child decrease his dosage slowly, and deal with any unpleasant side effects.

We know that with this short appendix, we may have left you with more questions than we answered. Let us encourage you to do thorough research and talk to experts in the fields of child psychiatry, child neurology, or developmental neurology. Find out all you can about alternative forms of treatment and, above all, get consistently biblical counseling from your pastor or one of the resources listed in Appendix B.

The choices you make about your child's care are very serious, and the repercussions may be long lasting. Ask the Lord to give you guidance as you seek to make informed decisions and trust that He will guide your thoughts.

Appendix D
Reasonable Expectations Chart

Your Expectation	Bible Reference	Personalize It	Consequences
Curfew	1 Thessalonians 5:7		
Entertainment	Romans 13:14		
Respectful speech and attitudes	Ephesians 6:4		
Participation in worship	Joshua 24:15		
Treatment of siblings	Matthew 7:12		

Your Expectation	Bible Reference	Personalize It	Consequences
Substance abuse	Proverbs 20:1		
Diligence in school and work	Proverbs 6:6,9-11		
Contribution to the family	Proverbs 10:5		
Diligence in responsibilities	Proverbs 6:6,9-11		
Dress and grooming	Deuteronomy 22:5; 1 Timothy 2:9		
Honesty	Ephesians 4:25		

Notes

―✑―

Introduction: My Dream Family

1. Parenting is such a significant responsibility that a father's failure to properly parent his children may disqualify him from leading in the church, as 1 Timothy 3:4-5 teaches: "He must manage his own household well, with all dignity, keeping his children submissive, for if someone does not know how to manage his own household, how will he care for God's children?"

Chapter 1—Why Do Kids Turn Out the Way They Do?

1. See also Proverbs 10:5; 19:26; 28:24; 29:3.
2. John MacArthur, from a May 17, 2004 letter to supporters of MacArthur's radio ministry "Grace to You."

Chapter 2—Their Choices, Our Tears

1. If you'd like to study more about conquering your fears, let us recommend Elyse Fitzpatrick's book *Overcoming Fear, Worry and Anxiety* (Eugene, OR: Harvest House Publishers), 2001.
2. Some parents become angry with God. They complain that they have sought to raise their kids according to the Scriptures, and that they have made significant sacrifices to do things right. Why didn't God bless their efforts? Why did God let this happen to them? "After all I have done for the Lord is this all the thanks I get?"

   Anger against God is never justified. The person who is angry with God wrongly believes God didn't treat him fairly. He is upset that God didn't do what he wanted, and when he wanted it done. It is always sinful to accuse God of being unjust. God is always just and fair. All that we and our children *deserve* from Him is wrath. What we have received instead is His goodness and mercy. He doesn't owe us good kids or a life free from suffering. Furthermore, He alone is all-wise. It is arrogant for us to try to tell Him what to do. We must trust that His agenda is perfect. He uses trouble for good (Genesis 50:20; James 1:2-4). He knows the blessings He has planned for us. Isaiah 41:11 says, "Behold, all who are incensed ['angered' NASB] against you shall be put to shame and confounded; those who strive against you shall be as nothing and shall perish." Romans 11:34-35 says, "For who has known the mind of the Lord, or who has been his counselor? Or who has given a gift to him that he might be repaid?" And Psalm 115:3 tells us, "Our God is in the heavens; he does all that he pleases." Even when terrible things happen and we are perplexed by what God is doing, we must be humble. Recall Job's words and his reaction after he lost his children and his property: " 'Naked came I from my mother's womb, and naked shall I return. The LORD gave, and the LORD has taken away; blessed be the name of the LORD.' In all this Job did not sin or charge God with wrong" (Job 1:21-22).

Chapter 3—Your Divided House

1. The Unique Challenges of a Spiritually Divided Marriage

We know that it's hard enough to deal with a wayward child when the husband and wife are spiritually united, but some Christian parents face the far greater challenge of raising a rebellious teen with an unbelieving partner or ex-spouse. In these cases the believer should strive to do everything she can to find common ground with the unbelieving parent. Most unbelievers want their kids to stay away from substance abuse and other dangerous behavior, and perhaps this is where common ground can be found for mutual support and control of your child. Often, however, there is a conflict of standards in which the unbelieving parent is more permissive. In the worst cases, the unbelieving parent may become an ally of the rebellious child and encourage her in worldliness, as many parents have experienced: "Our daughter rotated back and forth between two households with very different standards, and I believe that was a major factor in her rebellion."

Jesus told us to expect spiritual warfare in our families (Luke 12:52). Just as you have had to learn that you cannot control your child's heart, you cannot control the other parent, either. But you *can* lay your burdens before the Lord in prayer and take every opportunity to influence your children for the truth. You can also seek out guidance and support at your local church, asking an elder or mature Christian friend or biblical counselor to help you know how to wisely respond to the difficulties in your home. In the end, however, you'll be in the same place as those with strong and spiritual marriages: We all have to entrust the results to the Lord and believe that He will be faithful to us and our children.

Chapter 5—Fruit Inspection 102

1. Lewis, C. S., *The Lion, the Witch and the Wardrobe,* in The Chronicles of Narnia (New York: HarperCollins Publishers, 1950), p. 126.
2. Adult children living in the home should be subject to similar rules as a condition of remaining under their parents' roof.
3. Minors living in your home do not have the legal right of ownership. Although you do want to respect their privacy, as far as it is kind and wise for you to do so, you do have both the biblical and legal right to search their belongings and

confiscate anything that is harmful or illegal. In fact, you may be legally liable if you fail to do so.

4. A Web page that gives excellent movie reviews from a Christian perspective is Christian Spotlight on Entertainment (www.christiananswers.net/spotlight/home.html).

5. Several Internet-monitoring products are available, including Kid Defender and Spector.

6. Many kids have learned to clear the history on an Internet browser. Some kids have gone so far as to create hidden computer desktops and files.

7. We believe that even small children can be saved through faith in Christ (Mark 10:14).

8. Can your child lose his salvation? When the Bible speaks of ways to test our salvation, it is not teaching that people can lose their salvation. Rather, it is teaching that those who profess faith and fall away have not yet truly been born again, as in 1 John 2:19: "They went out from us, but they were not of us; for if they had been of us, they would have continued with us. But they went out, that it might become plain that they all are not of us." In Matthew 7:23, Jesus says of those who falsely professed faith, "I *never* knew you."

Sometimes the best step parents can take is to face reality. We know of parents whose adult son was living an openly immoral lifestyle with no interest in church or the things of God. A well-meaning friend sought to reassure them, saying, "You remember when he made a profession of faith when he was a child at camp. So at least you know he is going to heaven." But according to Scripture, it is much more likely this young man was never converted. The parents are probably living with a false hope. More importantly, they are missing out on opportunities to warn and evangelize their child.

Don't despair if it now seems to you that your child isn't really converted. You now have great opportunities to live out your faith in gentle witness and kind service, which may be what God uses to transform him.

Chapter 6—But My Child Is Different!

1. *Last One Picked, First One Picked On: Learning Disabilities and Social Skills with Rick LaVoie,* a video produced by WETA/PBS 1994.

2. Edward T. Welch, *Blame It on the Brain* (Phillipsburg, NJ: P & R Publishing, 1998), pp. 47-48.

3. Please refer to chapter 7 for explanations of these terms.

4. Tedd Tripp's *Shepherding a Child's Heart* (Wapwallopen, PA: Shepherd Press, 1995) is an excellent study of biblical child training. It contains three chapters on improving communication with your child.

Chapter 7—Will Medicine Help My Child?

1. For anxiety.

2. For ADHD.

3. For "crazy" thoughts and behavior.

4. Known as cognitive therapy. I do not recommend secular cognitive therapy to help challenged kids. I mention it in support of my position that there are

nonmedical "treatment approaches" that are recognized as effective even by secular doctors. I believe these treatments are effective because they are consistent with the Bible's teachings on the nature of man and how he changes, even though this is not the reason the creators of cognitive therapy give for why this method works.

5. I do not recommend this secular technique either, but cite it for the same reason as in the note above.

6. These are various ways to train the attention, not psychological therapies. I will discuss them later in this chapter. I do recommend these.

7. Often referred to as sensory integration therapy. It is a physical and not a psychological therapy.

8. See, for example, these two books by educational psychologist and educator Jane Healy: *Endangered Minds* (New York: Simon and Schuster, 1990), and *Failure to Connect: How Computers Affect Our Children's Minds and What We Can Do About It* (New York: Simon and Schuster, 1998).

9. The National Association of Nouthetic Counselors, a biblical counselor certifying and referral organization, maintains a list of biblical counselors. You can visit them at www.nanc.org.

10. Often called trichotillomania.

11. Often referred to as Tourette's syndrome.

12. This is the Laura Hendrickson "translation" of Philippians 4:6: "Do not be anxious about anything, but in everything by prayer and supplication with thanksgiving let your requests be made known to God."

13. Jeffrey Schwartz, MD, *Brain Lock* (New York: Regan Books, HarperCollins Publishers, 1996). I do not agree with Dr. Schwartz's specific way of helping with obsessions and compulsions, and I do not recommend this book for helping people with this problem. I cite it because of the evidence of brain change that is presented and associated with a change in thought and action patterns.

14. The term *neuroplasticity* refers to the brain's ability to change and develop throughout life. Neuroscientists no longer question whether the human brain is plastic, or changeable, throughout life. A large body of research over the last 40 years has demonstrated that, under the right conditions, the brain has a vast ability to modify itself in response to changing circumstances.

15. Some of this research is summarized in a challenging but readable book for laymen by Jeffrey Schwartz, MD, and Sharon Begley, *The Mind and the Brain* (New York: Regan Books, 2002). Dr. Schwartz has written this book to prove that man is a duplex being. He refers to the biblical "heart" as "mental force," and he attempts to reconcile his belief in Buddhism with his belief in evolution. Those of us who believe in a creator God have no need for his extensive discussion of quantum physics, although it should be interesting for the more scientifically oriented reader. But he uses scientific research to make a case for his belief that man is more than his material body. I highly recommend it for this purpose.

Christians don't have to wait for secular science to confirm what we already know to be true from God's Word. But we also don't need to be intimidated by those who would tell us that our approach is "unscientific," either.

As we discussed in chapter 6, "science" does not disagree with a biblical approach. It is an *interpretation* of scientific data based upon materialistic beliefs that disagree with the Bible's teachings on the nature of man, what causes his problems, and what can be done to solve them.

16. For the latest information on this subject, visit www.fda.gov/cder/antidepressants/default.htm.

17. Current research suggests that schizophrenia is probably due to an infection we are not yet able to diagnose, or some kind of brain damage, perhaps occurring before birth.

18. A disturbance in brain function that is transient, or temporary, resolves when the underlying condition causing it resolves, as when a person who is delirious with fever gets better on antibiotics, or when a brain tumor is removed. But there is no cure yet for what doctors call *primary* brain diseases that produce cognitive deterioration, hallucinations, and difficulty perceiving reality correctly, such as Alzheimer's disease or schizophrenia. Medicines in these cases may *suppress* the symptoms, but they cannot cure them.

19. This kind of training enables some developmentally disabled children who do not speak or understand language to acquire it. It helps those who have some language to develop vocabulary and concepts that are too difficult for them to learn by observation and imitation alone. It also teaches physical and school skills. Participating in this training improves attention and behavior.

Chapter 8—The War for Their Souls

1. In a very helpful book, father and biblical counselor Lou Priolo identifies 25 ways in which parents provoke their children to anger. See Lou Priolo, *The Heart of Anger* (Amityville, NY: Calvary Press, 1997).

2. Of course, if he is sinfully abusive, she should report this to her pastor (if he's a Christian) or to the police if he's not.

3. If dad is unwilling, them mom can. For more on family worship, see *Rediscovering the Lost Treasure of Family Worship* and *Teach Them Diligently* (see Appendix B).

Chapter 9—The Discipline Offensive

1. Tedd Tripp, *Shepherding a Child's Heart* (Wapwallopen, PA: Shepherd Press, 1995).

2. As children reach their mid-teens, measures other than spanking are probably more effective. If a young adult is getting out of control, it may be impractical to apply physical discipline, since the situation may turn into a brawl. Spanking (and the possible resultant scuffle) may also put the parents at a severe disadvantage if the authorities become involved.

3. Check with your cable or satellite provider for blocks that can be placed on certain stations.

4. You might be wondering what you'll do if your child refuses to submit to your rules. We'll answer that question in chapter 11.

5. Citing Winston Churchill, Speech before the House of Commons, June 4, 1940.

6. Enhanced Strong's Lexicon, Libronix Digital Library System.

Chapter 10—The Love Offensive

1. The expression "Love Offensive," is used in Jack Miller's *Come Back Barbara* (Phillipsburg, NJ: P & R Publishing), 1997.
2. The only sin that won't be forgiven is blasphemy against the Holy Spirit. Only God has the right to declare what sins against His person may not be forgiven. Since none of us are in the place of God, there should not be any sin we refuse to forgive.
3. For more information about this wonderful group and their ministry, go to the Web site www.momsintouch.org.

Chapter 11—"This, Our Son, Is Stubborn and Rebellious"

1. Galatians 5 tells us very clearly that those who practice this type of lifestyle will not inherit the kingdom of God (Galatians 5:19-21).
2. For instance, some parents who subscribe to certain methods of child-rearing may think that their child is incorrigible when, in actuality, it is the parents' demands that are out of line. Before you decide to send your child away or think of him as being incorrigible, please be sure that you've gotten consistently biblical counseling.
3. In California, a child can apply to the court to be emancipated from his parents while he is still a minor. Parents, however, cannot emancipate themselves from their minor children. If your child has run away and you don't know where he or she is, then you will want to contact a lawyer or a legal aid society to discover the laws about your responsibility should he or she get into trouble.

Chapter 12—Your Great Hope

1. Christian History Institute, Glimpses of the Faith #28, John Newton. Used by permission.
2. For information on St. Augustine's conversion and the faith of his mother, Monica, you can access http://www.gospelcom.net/chi/GLIMPSEF/Glimpses/glmps074.shtml.
3. "Graham was the stereotypical preacher's kid. His father was away for weeks at a time on evangelistic crusades when he was a child, and Franklin Graham strained against the Christian upbringing his mother, Ruth, was trying to instill in him.

   "He smoked, drank and took up fast motorcycle riding. He preferred camping and hunting in the mountains near their home in Montreat, N.C., to going to class. He came close to flunking out of a private high school in New York and got into fights in his public school in North Carolina. He learned to fly and was expelled from Christian college after taking a date on an overnight trip in a rented plane.

   "As a young adult, he struggled with what he felt were the demands of Christianity on his life. While on a trip helping missionaries in the Middle East, he found himself alone in a hotel room in Jerusalem, where he committed his life to Christ. He was 22." Quoted from "Franklin Graham Comes to Roanoake Valley for 3-Day Evangelistic Rally," *The Roanoake Times,* Sunday, April 27, 2003.

Appendix C: The Doctor Says My Child Needs Medicine

1. We are citing popular books for reference in this section, where possible, to provide the easiest access for parents who want to read more. Each of these popular-style references contains hundreds of additional references to scientific studies that back up their claims.
2. See Peter Breggin, MD, *The Antidepressant Fact Book* (Cambridge, MA: Perseus Publishing, 2001), pp. 27-42 and 67-69, and Joseph Glenmullen, MD, *Prozac Backlash* (New York: Simon and Schuster, 2000), pp. 57-59 and 94-100.
3. Sidney Walker III, MD, *A Dose of Sanity* (New York: John Wiley & Sons, 1996), p. 91.
4. See for example the entry for Paxil in *Physician's Desk Reference 2004* (Montvale, NJ: Thomson PDR, 2004), p. 1594.
5. Dr. Joseph Glenmullen thinks they may. See *Prozac Backlash*, pp. 12, 85-88.
6. *Prozac Backlash*, pp. 94-105.
7. You can view this information online at www.mca.gov.uk.
8. You can view the latest information on this subject at www.fda.gov/cder/drug/antidepressant/default.htm.
9. Gardiner Harris, "FDA Panel Urges Stronger Warnings on Antidepressants," *New York Times*, September 15, 2004.
10. FDA Talk Paper T04-08, March 22, 2004. You can view this paper on the FDA website at www.fda.gov/cder/drug/ antidepressant/default.htm.
11. *Prozac Backlash*, pp. 30-48.
12. Melissa Garland and Peter Kirkpatrick, "Atomoxetine Hydrochloride," *Nature Reviews*, Volume 3, May 2004, pp. 385-86.
13. According to the Formal Observation of Concerta versus Strattera (FOCUS), an unpublished study funded by the makers of Concerta. You can read about this at www.pharmalexicon.com/medicalnews.php?newsid=11655.
14. C.A. Zarate and M. Tohen, "Double-blind comparison of the continued use of antipsychotic treatment versus its discontinuation in remitted manic patients," *American Journal of Psychiatry*, Volume 161(1), January 2004, pp. 169-71.